GW00838524

Heal and Forgive II

"Nancy Richard's latest book reminds us that wisdom born of pain and struggle is true wisdom. She has the ability in sharing her story to engage others with similar experiences and in ways that give insight and direction. We are indebted to Richards for sharing her strength and courage with us. Again she helps us realize the limitations and capacities of the human heart and gives us hope that adequate healing from violence in families may be possible. I recommend this book to any survivor struggling with the brokenness that an abuser can do to a family. May truth help to heal the wounds and soften the scars."

—**Rev. Dr. Marie M. Fortune**, Founder and
Senior Analyst, FaithTrust Institute

"In *Heal and Forgive II*, Nancy Richards picks up where *Heal and Forgive* left off, taking us through the aftermath of divorcing a parent, to arriving at the acceptance that allows us to heal and move on to a new life.

"Whether you regard the idea of a family reunion with eager anticipation or numbing dread, *Heal and Forgive II* is a must-read. I would not advise anyone to even consider reconciliation without educating themselves on the pitfalls as well as the victories they might expect, and how to handle each one. In sharing her experiences, Nancy Richards gently guides us through the confusing jumble of conflicting thoughts, feelings, fears, and hopes involved in a possible reconciliation with our abusive families. *Heal and Forgive II* will educate you about the aspects of reconciliation you never even thought of, assist you in processing and understanding each one, and help you decide how to proceed next. An essential resource before taking that first step toward reconciliation, and an invaluable reference for every step along the way."

—Sister Renee Pittelli, Director, Luke 17:3 Ministries For Adult Daughters of Abusive, Controlling, and Abandoning Birth-Families

"Richards offers a gripping and revealing piece of work. *Heal and Forgive II* brings new meaning to the act of forgiveness. The author takes us on her journey from surviving horrific abuse to becoming a successful advocate on the subject of healing. I was moved by the similarities of our childhoods. I too, was a victim of child abuse and am comforted that I am not alone in my struggle to make peace with my past. Nancy illustrates the importance of validation, self-love and self-protection. Since reading her books, I am now on the right road to recovery."

—Leona Idom, survivor

Heal and Forgive II

The Journey from Abuse and Estrangement to Reconciliation

NANCY RICHARDS

Foreword by
Mark Sichel, CSW

Blue Dolphin Publishing

Copyright © 2008 Nancy Richards
All rights reserved.

Published by Blue Dolphin Publishing, Inc.
P.O. Box 8, Nevada City, CA 95959
Orders: 1-800-643-0765
Web: www.bluedolphinpublishing.com

ISBN: 978-1-57733-220-6

Library of Congress Cataloging-in-Publication Data

Richards, Nancy, 1957–
   Heal and forgive II : the journey from abuse and
estrangement to reconciliation / Nancy Richards ; foreword
by Mark Sichel.
      p. cm.
   Includes bibliographical references.
   ISBN 978-1-57733-220-6 (pbk. : alk. paper)
  1. Richards, Nancy, 1957– 2. Child abuse—United States—
Case studies. 3. Victims of family violence—United States—
Case studies. 4. Adult child abuse victims—United States—
Case studies. 5. Forgiveness. 6. Alienation (Social psychology)
7. Reconciliation. I. Sichel, Mark. II. Title.

   HV6626.52.R54 2008
   362.76'4092—dc22
   [B]

   2008021006

"A Visit with Me," from *Cherishing: Poetry for Pilgrims
Journeying On*, Copyright © 2007 Janice Gray Kolb.
Used by permission of Blue Dolphin Publishing

Printed in the United States of America

5   4   3   2   1

Dedication

*To the many men and women in estrangement support groups
who offer love and support to other individuals
while sharing their own journey,
and to those who are still suffering in silence…*

Contents

Foreword

Heal & Forgive II continues Nancy Richards' extraordinary struggle to heal the wounds of family abuse and estrangement. She candidly shares the horrors of her childhood and the challenge of family estrangement that she's had to learn to live with as an adult. Her story is gripping and compelling. Richards touches the reader's heart as she relates her endurance and stamina in the face of horrifying ill treatment and cruelty. She manages to avoid sensationalism by focusing on the repertoire of virtues she called upon to survive and heal. Her spiritual approach to healing involves forgiveness, generosity, hope, faith, strength and turning to a Higher Power as an overriding principle of recovery. Nancy has not only managed to carry on and thrive despite the cruelty she endured, she makes meaning out of her experience by giving the reader unbounded hope that compassion and kindness will help overcome even the worst family dysfunction and malevolence.

Heal & Forgive II is an important addition to the body of literature that addresses healing from family rifts. Despite being an "expert" in this subject, I am always in need of the collective wisdom shared by a community of survivors. Richards adds to each of our efforts to garner hope, wisdom and support to create lives of loving relationships unclouded by an abusive childhood.

For example, as a survivor of a seemingly permanent family estrangement, I was shocked when I reconciled with my father after I learned he was dying of leukemia. The illness had humbled him I thought, and I plunged back into a family dynamic that always left me bloody. I wish I had read *Heal & Forgive II* before I invited the abuse back into my life, because Nancy's wisdom about reconciliation would have grounded my illusion that my family had changed and protected me from the trauma that I inadvertently invited back into my life.

Nancy shares her struggles with reconciliation and shares her powerful feelings of fear, euphoria, disappointment, rejection and, finally, acceptance. She advises the reader to go slowly when there is an opportunity for reconciliation and that was precisely the advice that this expert needed to follow. Her conclusion throughout her journey is that forgiveness is the only way that healing can take place.

After attempting to reconcile with my family, I once again needed to heal. Nancy's wisdom has become a compass to navigate my endless recovery. The author's authenticity as she relates her challenges and set-backs will help any reader soothe their soul as they slowly move forward in healing from their particular trauma.

Nancy is guided by a demand on herself to act in a way that is correct and virtuous. She reminds the reader that gratitude and hope can sustain the reader's challenge in navigating the minefield of each of our own family cut-offs. In her generosity and authenticity she makes meaning of her own experience and inspires us to balance our efforts to reach out to our families while protecting ourselves from further abuse.

I had hoped I could create a memory of my father as a man who offered love, strength and integrity. I wanted this for myself as well as my children. He had on rare occasions overcome his fragility, and dying seemed to bring out the best in him with which to create positive memories. For a moment in time that was the case, but during a period of remission his true colors showed again and my father was poisoned by his rage, envy and hatred that characterized him for most of my life. I had hoped he could die at peace knowing he had repaired the rift that divided us for most of my life. He couldn't.

As I read the pages of this inspirational book, Nancy's hope, strength and wisdom helped me sustain my belief that I had done the correct thing in deciding to reconcile and forgive. She helped to shore up my faltering belief that I would have regretted not going through that last window—and sweetened my disappointment with the knowledge I had done the right thing. Equally important, my actions and correctness benefited my children who loved their grandfather, yet could never understand his capacity to arbitrarily explode and act with cruelty. *Heal & Forgive II* serves as a reminder that my gratitude and good fortune in my family of creation far outweighs the flaw in my family of origin.

Unlike many authors who write on this subject, Nancy does not need to quantify the severity of the abuse; she makes it clear that the overriding element of emotional and psychological damage is devastating no matter how the abusiveness manifested itself.

She touches the hearts of all of us whose abusive childhood has reached its defining moment in a loved one banishing us from what we have always known to be family.

Richards then takes the reader by the hand and helps us re-write the defining moment in our lives by showing us how forgiveness can unlock the gates to freedom and serenity. Ultimately that is the only way anyone can survive a family cut-off and craft a life steeped in serenity and uncondi-tional love for the loved ones who remain in our lives.

Perhaps the worst scarring of growing up with abuse is how it remains rooted in our psyches and becomes a bar-rier to fully enjoying life with the strength and wisdom of not allowing anyone's abusiveness to enter into our life. Nancy refuses to allow herself to re-create the hurtfulness and emotional violence of her childhood in her adult life, and she gives the reader hope and wisdom as she takes us through her process of healing. Her refusal to perpetuate the abuse is fired by struggling to sort out the various as-pects of being a virtuous human being. Nancy manages to exorcise her demons as much as any abuse survivor can. She moves the reader by declaring her newfound entitle-ment to harness constructive thoughts and action. She impressively models the moment-to-moment joy of being a loving and alive human being guided by gratitude, hope, generosity and confidence in her faith in a Higher Power.

The important part of Nancy Richards' story is that she transcended her mother's failures and flaws by finding compassion and forgiveness within herself. I presume her story will help all of us live more happily and fully as we create our own abuse-free lives.

Mark Sichel, LCSW, author, *Healing from Family Rifts: Ten Steps to Finding Peace After Being Cut Off from a Family Member*

Preface

Call it a clan, call it a network, call it a tribe, call it a family.
Whatever you call it, whoever you are, you need one.
—Jane Howard, *Families*

After a lifetime of abuse and betrayal, the day came when I reached the end of my endurance. I walked away from my mother, and embarked on a healing journey. After "divorcing" my mother, each of my family members—one by one—severed their relationships with me.

For more than a decade, I struggled with healing and forgiving those who caused my abuse. I shared my journey with the publication of *Heal and Forgive: Forgiveness in the Face of Abuse.*

Following a fourteen-year estrangement, much to my shock and disbelief, my family and I reunited.

Reconciliations can bring joy, excitement and a sense of awe like that of a miracle. At the same time, reunions can be frightening, stressful, fragile, and wrought with many pitfalls. Rebuilding relationships requires a great deal of emotional work and a willingness for each family member involved.

As unfair as it may seem, we have no control over the choices, desires, behavior or emotional progress of other individuals included in our family fracture. We can only affect a change within ourselves.

One of the several changes that helped me reconcile with my family were the many years I had spent healing enough to let go of my anger and forgive my abuser. I no longer needed validation, acceptance, and help from my family. I also learned to respond in a healthy manner, even when old unhealthy family patterns erupted.

I don't think one can experience the joy of reconciliation without first expressing the pain of estrangement—the cause of the rift—and the growth that must happen in order to reunite. When reconciling with a family member who shows remorse, the temptation is to deny or minimize old trauma. However, it is important to stand firmly in the truth. Accepting and making peace with the truth of the past illuminates the miracle of genuine reconciliation.

For me, this book begins with Chapter Five: Standing in the Truth. Although I didn't fully know it at the time I lived this chapter, I was at a crossroads in my life. The difficult choice I made to "divorce" my mother that year put me on a path towards authentic healing. That awakening is where this story really begins.

I was reluctant to write the first four chapters of this text, because I did not wish to revisit the painful period of my life encompassed in the beginning of the book. However, it was necessary to go back and include some early information in order for the rest of the book to make sense. For this reason, I have included a few stories from *Heal and Forgive: Forgiveness in the Face of Abuse* along with some new information concerning my earlier life.

My mother and brothers each have experienced their share of suffering, grief, and sorrow. Although our collective family dysfunction and the abuse my brothers and I endured runs much deeper than I share on the pages of this book, what I do offer is a blueprint for my healing journey.

The following pages present a personal account of the abuse at the center of my family fracture, the effects of estrangement, and the steps necessary to heal sufficiently in order to explore the possibility of reuniting. I have also included a final chapter to share what I have learned about reconciliation.

Most of my life, I felt alone. If you are a survivor of abuse, and/or estrangement, most likely you have felt alone as well. In this age of technology, all one needs to do is search the web for child abuse and estrangement recovery sites to understand that we are not alone! On the contrary, millions of survivors are seeking and searching for answers to quiet the pain of abuse and estrangement.

As a recovery seeker, I have soaked up as much information as possible to view life through a new lens—not the lens that was provided to me in childhood, but the one I needed to create for myself. It is my hope that you will find pieces of your own story in the pages of this book that offer validation, comfort, and a roadmap for healing and placing your own well-being first, no matter where that journey takes you.

Acknowledgments

Although I've felt alone many times in my life, writing this book was not a lonely experience. On the contrary, this book could not have been accomplished without the help and support of many others.

I would especially like to thank Alice Peppler, Paul Clemens, Leona Idom, Chris Richards, Bill Petschl, Mary Morrison, Dawn McArthur, and Colin McArthur for their careful reading of the manuscript. I'm grateful for their editing, knowledge, support, input, expertise, and helpful suggestions.

CHAPTER ONE

Kaleidoscope of Emotion

The Chinese use two brush strokes to write the word "crisis."
One brush stroke stands for danger; the other for
opportunity. In a crisis, be aware of the danger—
but recognize the opportunity.
—John F. Kennedy, Speech in Indianapolis, April 12, 1959

On an ordinary morning in the autumn of 2006, fourteen years after I had last spoken to my mother, my receptionist buzzed my office. Jan interrupted my busy morning with the cautiously spoken words, "There is a woman on line two who says her name is Jean Richards."

"Oh, oh," I surmised out loud, "she must have read my book."

I drew in a deep breath, preparing myself for the expected angry rant. I would merely convey to my mother my understanding for why she was upset, tell her that I loved her, and end the conversation with a gentle "good-bye." Certain I was prepared for our exchange, I picked up the phone. I wasn't prepared for what I heard next.

"Hi, Honey; this is Mom," came the soft-spoken words that I thought I would never hear again.

Confusion quickly replaced my clear-headed mind. The apology she offered for my abuse, along with her love and a desire for reconciliation were directly opposite to everything I knew about my mother. I told her I was speechless and that I never anticipated she would call again. After sitting quietly for a few moments, I said, "No matter what happens between us, Mom, you have given me a wonderful and irreplaceable gift."

We talked for a short while and exchanged contact information before concluding our conversation. I hung up and wept.

For the rest of the day, my body was in the state of shock. My thinking was clouded, my resting pulse hovered at around 120 beats per minute, and a dull headache grew with intensity. I grappled to make sense of something that made no sense in the world as I had known it. I couldn't hold a clear thought as my feelings ran rampant. I experienced a kaleidoscope of emotions, wildly clashing in distorted colorful directions—shock … love … fear … relief … joy … sorrow … excitement … pain … calmness … stress … happiness … sadness ….

I loved my mother and had long since forgiven her. Could this be true? Could Mom and I really have a relationship now? Ultimately, I stopped seeing her. Had she forgiven me too?

* * * * *

I grew up in a beautiful colonial house in an intimate Seattle neighborhood. My two brothers—Rob and Randy—and I were good buddies, enjoying our neighborhood friends and our playful time at home together. Our life was steeped in family gatherings and tradition. As children, my parents were the center of our universe. Each evening they tucked us into our beds with a bedtime ritual and a good-night kiss. My parents involved us in many family and community activities, provided holiday magic and delighted in our mischievousness. I felt safe and loved.

Tragically, when I was nine, my dad died of a brain aneurysm. With him died my childhood and my safety with my mother. No longer did I enjoy the security of feeling loved; all of the passages mothers and daughters share were simply gone. There was, however, a new man in Mom's life. Year after year, my stepfather beat and tortured my brothers and me as my mother silently witnessed my abuse, defended my stepfather, and even participated in the abuse. Through all the violence and betrayal, I starved for and sought after my mother's love and protection.

Mom's marriage to Ed gave birth to a pattern that would take me decades to understand. I had glimpses of the mother I thought I knew when she was married to my father in between each husband; however, whenever she partnered with a mate, she took on the persona of the new man in her life and went to any lengths to safeguard her marriages. Often that meant sacrificing her children.

Dad had been a man of deep faith. He was family-oriented, and had a zest for life. Together, Mom and Dad provided a sense of fun and security. When my mother remarried, the household and child-rearing rules were dictated by a violent newcomer—my stepfather, Ed.

At ten years of age, the first morning as a new family was quite memorable for me. Mom had warned us the night before that, contrary to the old ways with our father, the master bedroom would be off limits to us. There would be no running in and out, no morning greeting or playing games. Saturday morning, my brothers and I played peacefully in Rob's bedroom, anxiously waiting for Mom and Ed to wake up and start what we thought would be our exciting new life together.

Suddenly, the door of the master bedroom flew open! Ed moved quickly down the hall while our grim-faced mother appeared in Rob's doorway. "Ed is very angry with you for making too much noise," she said.

We had neither been fighting nor yelling and we protested against being called "noisy."

Just then, Ed appeared in the doorway to Rob's room holding a wooden paddle from one of our games in his hand. With face muscles tight, he turned to my youngest brother.

"Randy," he directed sharply, "grab your ankles!"

To my amazement and horror, just as my five-year-old brother's little hands clenched tightly around his ankles, a tremendous crack broke the uncomfortable hush that lingered in the room. Randy jumped into the air, clutched his buttocks, and ran to his room, screaming in pain and surprise.

Undisturbed, Ed commanded Rob to grab his ankles in a harsh voice.

As if hypnotized into submission, my eleven-year-old brother complied. Ed swung his arm back, and another loud crack resounded through the air. He hit Rob with such force that the paddle broke, flew across the room, crashed into the wall, and clattered noisily to the floor. Rob's face turned red. He averted his eyes as he fled to his bed.

Without missing a beat, Ed turned to me, and said in a voice void of emotions, "I am very angry I have to use my hand on you. It isn't fair for me to hurt my hand because you are a bad child. Grab you ankles, Nancy."

He hit my ten-year-old frame so hard I barely kept from losing my balance and crashing on my face. I ran to my room in tears. My bottom was on fire. My mind raced to figure out just what happened—so quickly and so violently. What had we done? Why this kind of cruel punishment? For what? What could I do to prevent this from happening again?

In the safety of my room, I hovered gingerly on the edge of my bed, my buttocks stinging from the blow. I thought about what just had happened. In my short ten years, never had I heard anybody talk about anything like this. Little did I know at the time, this incident would pale in comparison with what the future held for me.

Later in the day, I approached my mother hoping to find solace. Mom told me that Ed found us ill behaved— "the worst kids he had ever seen."

"Nobody else has ever told us that we are terrible children," I challenged my mother in a hurt and passionate voice.

Mom looked at me crossly. "Ed said that your father spoiled you and you have terrible manners. He said he is going to whip you into shape. And," she added firmly, "I am grateful for his help."

I was hurt and confused.

Ed relieved his tension by punishing us for the most obscure rules of the day and Mom stood by as he beat us with a wooden paddle or with his fists.

After a stressful day at work, Ed raced for my closet to check the heels of my shoes. Once he discovered they were unevenly worn, he beat me with the paddle to teach me to walk straight.

No matter how hard we tried to stay out of his way, Ed found or invented almost daily transgressions of his rules that would warrant the use of severe punishment. After a while, all he had to do was look at one of us and issue a curt "Grab 'em!" and our young and slender backs would bend round, grasping tiny ankles, anticipating the painful and cruel moment when the hard piece of wood would connect forcefully with a burning backside and send shock waves up our spines.

Sitting down on my bruised behind after the routine beatings was more than painful, but the emotional impact of the blows far exceeded the physical pain. Long after our tender bottoms healed, our hurt feelings continued to bleed. They turned to acid, corroding and corrupting our hearts and souls.

Mom watched in silent acquiescence. After the loss of Dad, Mom immediately sought to shelter her insecurities and fears under the mantle of remarriage — a man to run her business affairs, a man to take over, to take control of what she considered her runaway life. This came first.

On Saturdays we couldn't go out into the neighborhood to play until we passed room inspection. Although we kept our rooms according to the enlisted men's journal of procedure—with socks rolled just so, underwear folded a certain way, shirts and sweaters in a meticulous row, all hangers in the closet pointing in the same direction, and every spot in our rooms at inspections status, we never passed weekly inspection and were punished accordingly.

One Saturday, I was sure I would pass room inspection and get to go out to play. Ed entered my room with a smile as he began his forensic search. Moving slowly from one area to the next, his body revealed his frustration, as he was unable to find an infraction. Ed's back and shoulders stiffened while the veins in his neck started to bulge. With his back facing me, I stood at attention as Ed opened and shut each one of my dresser drawers in quiet desperation. Suddenly, calm washed over his body like a wave. Fear gripped me as his face lit up with sadistic triumph. He wrapped a white handkerchief around his finger and headed for my bed. I watched in disbelief as he lifted the bedspread and ran his finger down the bed slat encasing the mattress. With a smug smile, he uttered in disgust, "Dust! Goddamn, Nancy, if you can't do a job right, don't do it at all."

"Okay! I won't," I snapped furiously.

In a flash, Ed threw me across the bedroom! My back hit the wall with a thud, knocking the wind out of me. I bounced to the hardwood floor.

When my mother refused to help me, I turned to others for aid. There was neither understanding nor encouragement whenever I tried to talk to outsiders of what went on at home. On the contrary: "You should obey your stepfather." "You should try to understand your mother." "How can you be so selfish?" "Look at all you have."

Puzzled and shocked, I whirled in a vicious circle. If I never told anyone, the abuse would never stop. If I did tell, insult was added to injury when my chosen confidant supported Mom and Ed.

Few things darken a child's heart more than to live without hope.

Most families use the dinner hour as a time to talk about the events of the day, acknowledge each other, make plans, and in general, be together. That was not the case in our household. Dinner was a scheduled nightmare giving Ed the unopposed opportunity to come up with surprise acts of cruelty.

There was not one meal when one of us wasn't routinely terrorized or abused. With unerring regularity, Ed would jab a fork into one of our tender arms or the backs of our hands. My brothers and I went to great lengths to avoid sitting next to Ed during mealtime. On many occasions he doubled up his fists and knocked us off our chairs. Overtaken by surprise, our seats tipped back and tossed us onto the hard kitchen floor.

I questioned how my mother could grant her approval when my stepfather burned my ten-year-old hands. Or, how she nonchalantly ate her meal, never looking up from her plate when Ed commanded my brother Randy to jab himself with a fork.

There was no peaceful moment to be had when Ed was around. Fear stalked our hearts and souls. Impending doom loomed permanently behind a door, in a corner of a room, and in our minds. It was the only sure thing we could rely on.

Ed threw us down the stairs, ridiculed us and tortured our bodies and minds. We all suffered regular beatings; however, Ed targeted Rob most frequently and brutally.

From behind a closed door or another part of the house, the often-heard agonizing screams from my brothers created an unbearably helpless feeling within me, and paralyzed me in mute despair. At times, Ed's beatings were so violent that I feared one of us might die.

Yet, the physical abuse we survived at the hands of my stepfather paled in comparison to the emotional damage I sustained from my mother. Each time I approached her for protection from Ed, she blamed me. She pulled me aside harshly with the words, "Why do I always have this trouble with you; only you—never the boys? You are sick, and a crazy troublemaker! Stop trying to make trouble and learn to get along."

Mom's words left me feeling useless and defeated.

Each night after an evening wrapped in fear, Mom would say to each of us kids, "Good night. I love you." I'd lie in bed frightened, doubting my own worth and trying to make sense of her words. What's wrong with me? Why am I so bad?

Long after physical injuries heal, the effects of emotional abuse lingers into and sometimes throughout adulthood. Emotional abuse is harder to explain and more difficult to identify because it leaves no physical scars, but rather is hidden away, ravaging our hearts and our souls.

Andrew Vachss is an attorney who has devoted his life to protecting children and youths who have been sexually assaulted, physically abused, or neglected. He is also a founder and national advisory board member of PROTECT: The National Association to Protect Children (http://www.protect.org/). In an August 1994 article in *Parade Magazine*, Vachss answers the often-asked question, "What is the worst case you ever handled?"

When you're in a business where a baby who dies early may be the luckiest child in the family, there's no easy answer. But I have thought about it—I think about it every day. My answer is that, of all the many forms of child abuse, emotional abuse may be the cruelest and longest-lasting of all.

Under Ed's military-style regime, my mother became more than just a quiet observer of his regular beatings of us kids. At times she was an active participant, going to any length to follow Ed's rules.

Ed's mother, Ethel, was a hard and humorless woman who obviously taught Ed his destructive methods. She dropped by the house one afternoon for an unexpected visit. Mom was embarrassed because I'd left some items lying out in the living room; the house wasn't at its usual inspection status. After settling Ethel into the kitchen, Mom called me into the living room and ripped into me for leaving my things lying around. An argument ensued which left me in tears. Disregarding my sobbing, Mom handed me a sweater Ethel had brought and asked me to go to the kitchen to thank her.

I remained behind for a moment trying to compose myself before thanking Ethel for the gift. Just as I was about to enter the kitchen, I overheard Ethel voice critical disapproval of my behavior. Mom didn't hesitate a moment. In order to comply with Ed's rules, she grabbed me by the arm and pulled me through the room until I was in front of Ethel. She commanded me to "Grab 'em!" and reached for the paddle, which always sat at the ready on the wall shelf.

The beating left me shocked and devastated, humiliated and feeling trapped in a lonely world of pain.

* * * * *

Frequently in abusive family systems, when the responsible party doesn't know how to take responsibility, it is common for a parent to use the "divide and conquer" method of control to maintain "status quo." A scapegoat is chosen to carry the blame, shame, and responsibility in order for the rest of the family to escape personal pain and/or accountability. I was that scapegoat.

In *The Dance of Anger: A Woman's Guide to Changing the Patterns of Intimate Relationships*, Harriet Goldhor Lerner, Ph.D., states, "Focusing on a 'problem child' can work like magic to deflect awareness away from a potentially troubled marriage or a difficult emotional issue with a parent or grandparent."

My assignment as family scapegoat was firmly established at twelve years of age when I refused to play one of Ed's sadistic games.

Prior to the evening meal, we were playing a game on the living room floor. Whenever we were called to the table, we had learned to drop what we were doing and rush at top speed to our places at the table.

When the call to dinner came one evening, we were in a quandary. If we cleaned up the game and packed it away, our arrival at the table would be delayed —an unpardonable infraction punishable by a beating. If we didn't pick up the game and simply rushed to the table, we would be severely punished for not being orderly.

What to do?

We chose to rush to the table. There was no right in our lives; there was only wrong. Right became wrong, and nothing escaped Ed's eager eye. He glommed onto every opportunity or better yet, he created one. He glanced at the living room and saw the game board in the middle of the floor. Sure as rain, Ed had his case for the evening.

"You're slobs! I'm furious with you slobs. You didn't pick up your game. Careless, thoughtless slobs! I'll teach you a lesson. We'll play a new game you won't forget."

"Rob, Randy, Nancy," he continued a sadistic grin across his hard mouth, "you will form a circle in the living room. You'll all grab your ankles, and I'll hand Rob the paddle. Rob will hit Nancy as hard as he can." He looked piercingly at my brother.

"Rob," he continued, "if you don't hit Nancy hard enough, she gets the paddle and hits you as hard as she can. Then she'll turn to Randy and hit him as hard as she can. If you do hit each other hard enough, you keep passing on the paddle, and so on," he concluded his instructions with a vague motion of his hand.

"I will referee the game and make sure you're playing it right," he added smugly.

I started to shake all over as I listened to Ed explain what he referred to as the "Paddle Game." My breath was labored, and I was so terrified I couldn't control the tremor that spread over my limbs. How does he think up these games? He and his games are straight from hell, I thought wildly. I had recognized the sadistic pleasure he derived from tormenting the boys and me.

Enough! I had enough. It was one thing for Ed to beat us, but I wouldn't be a part of beating my brothers. I looked around the table. Mom had "left town." Ed appeared highly pleased with himself, and the boys looked frightened and, at the same time, compliant.

I stood up, "I won't play," I stated shakily. Then I burst into tears and fled to my room.

Mom appeared in my room after a while, and in a sort-of, matter-of-fact voice tried to assure me that she would have stepped in and not permitted Ed to conduct the paddle game. I didn't believe her. For the past two years, Mom had not stopped anything this man had done to us.

Before she left my room, Mom informed me she had decided to divorce Ed.

I felt both elated and worried at the same time. After all, for two years we had heard how much Mom and Ed cared for one another. We had also been told in no uncertain terms, that we were awful kids and were to blame for all the trouble the family endured. I was petrified that it would be my fault Mom's marriage ended in divorce.

Terrified of the consequences Mom's decision would have on me, and the load too heavy for my twelve-year-old psyche, I blurted out, "Mom, I know it is all my fault." Tears brimmed over in my eyes as I said, "I know that you and Ed would be happy together if it weren't for the problems the boys and I cause. I'm so sorry! I don't want you to be unhappy."

Mom readily agreed, "True! All we ever argue about is you kids. I love Ed."

Devastated at the enormity of my obvious shortcomings and my responsibility for my mother's happiness, I said, "Okay, Mom, I'll play the paddle game."

"It's too late, Nancy," Mom frowned. "Ed is packing his things. But you can go and ask him to stay."

For the sake of Mom's marriage and to rid myself of the responsibility for this mess, I trudged off to find Ed, who was in the master bedroom packing.

The tall man, who was unhurriedly stuffing things from a chest of drawers into a suitcase, stopped and straightened up when I entered the room. Without a preamble, without Hi or Hello, tears streamed down my face and I ran up to him, hugged the man I so desperately despised, and in a voice choked with emotion, I begged him to stay.

Ed, not wanting to appear too eager, grudgingly gave in to my pleas. Yes, he would stay, he grouchily acquiesced. I untangled my arms from reaching around him and left the room, numb and empty. I felt like a balloon with the air gone out, hovering aimlessly at low, so very low.

I now was the designated driver to steer the family's vehicle of all-around contentment on a safe course. I would have to stand up and try to prevent abuse, and take the blame if it didn't work. What a spot to be in. I felt little else but raw panic.

Rob raged at me mercilessly. "We could have been rid of the son-of-a bitch," he said hoarsely in the quiet of his room as he faced me. "You prevented that. What happens now will be your fault!" He was furious.

From then on, Rob blamed me for every temper tantrum Ed displayed, every beating, every battering, and the torrents of foul and nasty words directed at us.

Wracked with unimaginable guilt, I barely thought I would survive. In my lost and lonely world, I longed for safety, for understanding, comfort and love. Mostly, I longed for my father.

* * * * *

During my father's growing up years throughout the 1930s and 1940s, he spent his summers at his aunt's home on Lake Roesiger. In his free time, Dad delighted in every opportunity to be on the water by agreeing to row Mrs. Roesiger, parasol and all, around the lake. The lake captured his young heart and wouldn't let go. He vowed to buy a summer home of his own as soon as he had grown and he made good on his dream.

Mom shared Dad's love of our cabin on the lake and together they instilled within us kids that same love of our safe haven in the country, along with a warm sense of family history. It was Dad's wish that the whole family would enjoy the lake for generations to come.

We grasped every opportunity to escape to the peace and quiet of the house on the lake, surrounded by sheltering firs. The moment I walked up the steps to the porch of the cabin, a comforting, easy feeling of serenity and harmony settled over me.

Childhood memories of fun-filled days crowded every corner of the rustic cabin and brought back the precious moments that reflected the safety and love my father had for his children. From the past, I conjured up memories of my father and of my mother. As I pulled on my armor and braced myself for the battles I knew were waiting for me, these were the memories that kept my sanity.

* * * * *

To the outside world, we appeared to be the "All-American" family. We lived in an impeccable home, filled with all the amenities of the day, and attended our neighborhood church on a regular basis. Our family was well known at the local ski resort and we continued to participate in many community activities.

A confusing aspect to my relationship with my mother was that, at times, she could be quite charming. When we were little, Mom volunteered as a Cub Scout and Bluebird leader. She also provided us with music lessons, signed us up for sports and made sure that we took our studies seriously. Mom is an artist who especially liked to paint in oil. The year Dad died, she thrilled me with painting lessons. That first painting still hangs in my home today. She gave our home and our lives her own artistic signature by painting holiday murals on the windows, creating art out of nature or individualizing our pancakes with our initials as she cooked them for breakfast. Mom had a "goofy" side as well, sometimes singing off-key as she danced with us. And yet, I'd always do something bad to ruin our fun. The load of guilt and remorse I carried in my heart left room for little else. Oh, how I wished I was lovable.

* * * * *

At fifteen years of age—feeling helpless, angry, and spent—I attempted to find "outside" help by calling a teen-help hotline. After explaining the goings on at home, the volunteer suggested that I call the police.

I was elated when I hung up the phone. I had someone who listened, understood, and believed me. I had found somewhere to go, someone to fight my battle. I felt a strange surge of power and purpose. Nobody could hurt me anymore.

Filled with this new feeling of having rights and being somebody, I told Mom that the volunteer told me to call the police.

Mom's mouth fell open. Horrified, she blurted out, "Oh, my God, did you give them your name?"

I had hoped in vain that Mom would rush to my rescue and say something like: "Oh, dear God, Nancy, I'm so sorry for what you've been through. I'll put a stop to this at once; I'll help. I'll be there for you!"

Instead I heard her outcry of: "Oh dear! What will happen to me? What will the neighbors think?"

Another betrayal.

Finally, Mom asked me in a desperate voice to give her a few minutes to think it over. She disappeared into her bedroom. When she emerged a moment later, she announced that she had made arrangements for me with the parents of my good friend, Lori Anderson. It was summer vacation time. The Andersons were staying at their beach house, and I was invited to spend some time with them. Mom would take that interval to "straighten" things out. She would get rid of Ed.

I was thrilled. I loved my mother as most children love their mothers, and was ecstatic she was finally going to right this wrong.

Mom had informed the Andersons that I was having problems at home and everyone needed a break.

A few days later, Mom appeared at the Andersons unannounced and found me there alone. She demanded I return home.

"Is Ed still there?" I asked defiantly.

Mom replied, "Yes."

"Then I am not going home with you! I won't be hurt anymore," I said with fierce determination.

An argument ensued and much to my amazement, Mom flew into a rage and screamed, "You fucking little bitch. I never want to see you again as long as I live!"

She turned on her heels and walked towards the door in quick angry strides. Then abruptly stopped, looked back and threw a bottle of Valium at me and yelled, "Here! Take them. You need them. You're sick!"

If someone had asked me how I felt at that moment, I would not have found the words to describe my feelings. I was numb. The hateful words she had flung at me burnt to my core. I knew I had lost and was lost. I sat down and sobbed. How devastating to be hated by one's own mother.

In the meantime, Mom convinced family, neighbors and friends alike that she was the unfortunate mother of a deeply troubled child. Everyone apparently believed her. Meanwhile I suffocated under the heavy load of blame and shame, hopelessness and betrayal.

Three weeks later, Mom appeared again at the Andersons' home and informed me impassionately that she had asked Ed to go his way.

That was all I wanted to hear. Peace and warmth rolled over me like a soft blanket on a freezing day, as I looked gratefully at my mother. This was too good to be true. I hurriedly packed my few things, thanked the Andersons profusely for letting me stay, hugged Lori, and followed Mom to the car. She had redeemed herself in my eyes. Life would be wonderful again. Mom loves me after all.

A week after I had come home, Ed, smug and strutting with his victory, returned to the family fold and took up where he left off.

As a powerless child seeking protection from the adult bystanders in my life, I didn't recognize the look of fear behind the eyes of the grown-ups with whom I sought refuge. I didn't understand the apprehension that drove them to inaction.

From the isolated torment of my abusive childhood, I cried out to God and to the Universe, "Why will no one help me?"

I was an invisible youngster. I grew up alone and in emotional poverty, without being seen by anyone. I didn't have a voice; therefore, I had no value.

Nobody reported my childhood abuse—not my family therapist, not my doctor, my teachers, my family, friends, or neighbors. So many knew, but nobody helped.

CHAPTER TWO

Stumbling Forward

My brothers and I endured more than six years in the horrific labyrinth of beatings, torture, and betrayal, before my mother finally divorced Ed. Freed from years of physical violence at the hands of this man, I imagined that all of our troubles were over. I envisioned our family becoming the loving, happy unit that I remembered before my father's death.

We all thought that Ed was to blame for all of our family misery and with him out of the picture, we believed that our misfortune had come to an end. I quickly learned that we were mistaken.

I didn't anticipate the continuation of embedded abusive family patterns or the ways our still growing adolescent brains had been affected during our years of abuse. For the bulk of our childhood, my brothers and I were unprotected under a regime of severe physical and emotional violence. We continued to respond to life in direct correlation to our individual experiences.

Mom was blithely unaware of our needs and was guided by her own interests. She pursued her ambitions and pleasures, which were divided between working and dating. She wasn't around to bring the much-needed order and cohesiveness into our lives.

Without the necessary structure and safe place to call home, my life seemed out of control. I escaped reality in many different fashions. At night, in the quiet of my room, I dreamt of my father and of safety. When I was away from home, I was the "life of the party"—having extraordinary amounts of fun, while keeping the pain at bay. I spent much of my time at home, banishing my emotional self to a far-away, unreachable place. Other times at home, I stepped in as the family mother. Everyone was forever at each other's throat and I took upon myself the role of mediator.

I had a great deal of empathy for my family members. I especially hurt for my brothers. It was easier for me to deal with my own pain than it was to witness their anguish.

Surprisingly, I often succeeded in settling differences between Mom, Rob and Randy by "holding" and validating their experiences as well as my own. I expected them to reciprocate. Yet no one interceded on my behalf. I suffered alone and in silence, feeling blamed and misunderstood.

Feeling "unseen," like a woodpecker, I repeatedly begged Mom to understand my perspective—to hear me, see me, approve of me and understand me. It took me a lifetime to learn that, although empathy is a good thing, empathy should go hand-in-hand with clear, respectful boundaries. In other words—*feeling* empathy didn't mean I had to *act* on my empathy. When I offered that which I didn't receive, I became angry, resentful, and defensive. As a child, I should have received empathy from my mother. However, later as an adult, I needed to learn to *act* on my empathy only in mutual relationships.

I needed a mother as all young women do. The abandonment and rejection I felt left me hurting from the very depths of my soul. If Mom doesn't love me—who will?

Most everyone loves their mother and I was no exception. While society and family structure encourage boys to distance themselves from their mothers, girls are encouraged to pattern themselves after the woman who gave them life. Although I was very angry with her, I kept on loving her and needing her with child-like ardor, but at the same time, I was tortured by a dreadful sense of loss of "not really having a mother."

Drained and empty, I felt as if I existed in the confines of a deep and dark nothingness—an orphan of circumstances rather than a lonely child cheated by death.

Although my mother was very much alive and on the scene, she continually betrayed me and turned her back on me emotionally. This left me without the benefits of the intimacy so vital to the development of a young woman. I didn't have a role model; there was no one to look to for passing on that instinctive knowing, that certain wisdom that is a mother's legacy.

I didn't realize that the emotional connectedness a daughter desires from her mother was not a part of my mother's make-up. She didn't fit the societal motherhood mold. I needed a drink of motherly love so badly that I didn't realize I was seeking water from an empty well.

After the loss of my father, I lived with the hope and the longing that Mom would comfort me, as I had been comforted before he died. Although both of my parents provided childhood events and activities—I didn't realize that it was my father who made all the emotional connections I received. He was the one who shared his feelings and listened to mine.

My most heartfelt memories of my father are his loving eyes. His eyes gave me confidence as I ventured into my world. While I went soaring independently on my bike for the very first time, a look of pride, commensurate with what was obviously an unparalleled achievement, came across my father's face. Moreover, the sweet grin Dad displayed as we headed out the door to eat the dinner I prepared for the third-grade Father-Daughter Boxed Supper is fondly imprinted upon my mind. There is no greater legacy left to a child than a parent's loving gaze, a kind word or a warm embrace.

As a small child, I viewed my parents as a single unit. Because I was so young and I received all the love and nurturing I needed from my father, I "overlooked" my mother's emotional unavailability even while Dad was alive. I lived in denial—hoping to recapture the love I felt from my "parents."

The physical abuse my brothers and I endured during childhood and the betrayal of our mother was just the tip of the iceberg. It would be many years before I could see beyond it, to comprehend the extent of the emotional abuse my mother reserved just for me.

In fact, since I was a child, Mom told me that although she loved me, she didn't like me. She said that she preferred boys over girls. Mom hugged and cuddled the boys, while I was the lonely, lost bystander to her show of affection. I was starved for attention, but when I asked Mom why she never hugged me, she authoritatively stated, "Because, you don't like to be hugged."

I can't remember a time when the sharing of emotion was allowed. Mom often slapped me when I cried, or she grabbed me by the back of the neck and ran me in front of the mirror to say, "Look at how ugly you look when you cry."

I spent a lifetime seeking from my mother the emotional connection I didn't realize she never gave me to begin with—the love I received from my father.

* * * * *

By the time I was seventeen, Rob had moved into his own apartment, leaving Randy and me still at home. Exceptionally intelligent, Rob excelled academically, and musically as a concert violinist. His creative imagination is at times awe-inspiring. Rob's mischievous antics were infamous in our neighborhood. He was also quick to react from an angry, sometimes violent and unpredictable woundedness.

When Rob moved out on his own, he instituted the annual tradition of calling me on the anniversary of Dad's death. For the better part of the next two decades, I found Rob on the other end of the telephone each April 30th with the words, "Do you know what today is?"

"Yes," was my yearly reply. With those simple words, we acknowledged our connection to our father and our history. No further mention of Dad was required while we shared the latest events in our lives.

In a sad way, there are few encounters more comforting than to relate traumatic events with another individual who has shared the same experiences. In many respects, Rob was that individual for me. When Mom was married to Ed, Rob and I shared our misery over the cruelty that Ed perpetrated against us—experiences that no one else we knew could even fathom, let alone understand. Because we are close to the same age, when Dad died, Rob and I experienced his loss in a similar fashion. We shared each other's grief and understood each other's pain. However,

Rob vehemently protected Mom from any suggestion that she held even the slightest responsibility for our welfare.

Within months of her divorce from Ed, Mom had another new man in her life. Her soon-to-be third husband, Bill was a practicing alcoholic who set off all of my warning bells. Mom's persona changed again to align with Bill's rules and his unflattering opinions. Mom and I started quarreling bitterly. She told me flat out that Bill was her first priority and his treatment of me was inconsequential.

My observations and appraisals of him led me to warn Mom that he was all wrong. But she got angry with me for butting in on her life and told me I was cruel.

I knew it was starting all over again.

I escaped Bill's alcoholic conduct and Mom's indifference towards me by moving out of state, leaving Randy to his own devices. Randy often escaped his home life in the company of friends. He was sweet, charismatic and possessed an innocent quality that easily endeared him to almost everyone he met.

I finished high school in Morro Bay, California, where, along with my future husband, I rented a room in a nearby house. Morro Bay was considerably smaller than bustling Seattle and I was lonely. When it was time to graduate, I did so without family and fanfare.

Months after my arrival in California, I received the disappointing news that Mom and Bill had married. Mom's marriage to Bill resulted in the birth of my half-brother, Brandon, and hours of my concern on behalf of my mother and my two younger brothers. Any time I expressed my concern to my mother, brothers and grandmother over the telltale signs of abuse I witnessed on my visits home, the family accused me of constantly "stirring the pot" and became angry with me if I brought it up.

* * * * *

For quite a while I tucked away the past and made believe all was well in my world. I remembered only the good from my childhood and convinced myself I had a loving family back in Seattle.

After years of oppressive violence, I basked in my newfound freedom and in all the amazing choices life had to offer. I did not intend to look back.

Without the day-to-day presence of my family as a reminder, it seemed easy to forget past hurts and unwind in the safety of the present. But, no matter where I went, the past had a way of nipping at my heels. My trauma remained fused to me, no matter how hard I tried to ignore the pain. Post-traumatic flashbacks, depression, anxiety, fear—these were my companions from the past, and they hung over me like a dark cloud and crowded my mind.

Young and newly married, I walked blindly into motherhood with a burning desire to create a new loving family. I sought to provide all the affection that goes with a happy childhood, along with the warmth and closeness that makes family life secure and content.

I was crushed at my mother's response when my husband called her with the news that she had a lovely new granddaughter. She was disappointed; she had wanted grandsons. When she did speak to me, her only acknowledgment that I'd had a baby was, "Ha, Ha. No more bikinis for Nancy."

After my second child was born, Mom continued to ignore my children, both in infancy and as they grew. Her indifference to my daughters was one of the deepest pains I endured.

I was unaware at the time how damaged I was from years of abuse or that my abuse would affect my ability as a parent.

Looking back at my children's growing up years brings relief that I narrowly evaded disaster. My only saving grace was the basic awareness that I was mistreated and my willingness to attempt to heal. Fortunately, for my children and for me, although I entered motherhood without foresight, as soon as I realized I was pregnant, I devoured parenting books, took parenting classes, surrounded myself with people whose parenting skills I respected and admired, and drew off my earlier memories and experiences with my father. There was no conscious plan to "break the cycle," but fortunately, through hard work, luck and happenstance, these intentional choices on my part marked the beginning of breaking the cycle of family violence with respect to my own children.

Back in Seattle, although everyone denied the presence of abuse at Mom's house—it was true. The straw that ended Mom's marriage to Bill came one day when he was drunk. Mom relayed the incident to me during a quick recuperative visit to my house in California. She arrived weeks after my husband and I had our first-born daughter. My shell-shocked mother informed me that while she lay on the couch with eleven-month-old Brandon on her stomach, Bill began punching her in the face. She screamed, "The baby! The baby! You'll hurt the baby!"

Fourteen-year-old Randy ran down the stairs at the sounds of her screams and jumped on Bill's back. Amidst the violence, Mom yelled out to Randy to call the police. As Randy jumped off his back to turn for the phone, Bill ran and yanked it from the wall. In a panic, Randy ran outside and screamed from the front lawn, "Help! Help! Call the police!"

The police came, Mom and Randy left for Grandma and Grandpa's with Brandon in tow, and Mom filed for divorce.

When she finished with her story, Mom asked me, "How did you know Bill was an alcoholic?"

"It was just obvious, Mom."

She desperately pleaded with me, "You knew! Why didn't you convince me? Why didn't you prevent me from marrying him?"

"Are you kidding me, Mom?" I was incredulous. "That wasn't my responsibility. Besides, you were mad at me when I told you he was an alcoholic and you told me to "butt out." You complained to everyone in the family about me and they all told me to stop causing problems."

"Well, you were right and I'm going to wait a long time before I get married again. I was only seventeen when I married your dad," she continued, "I moved straight from my parent's house into your father's. My marriage to Ed came so soon after your dad died that I never had time to grieve his death. I was so naïve, I didn't even know there were bad people in the world. I also didn't know how to take care of a home and raise three small children on my own. I felt so lost; I needed help. Ed said he would help me and he turned out to be a monster. I didn't know how to cope with the situation. Then I married Bill so soon after Ed, I never had time to catch my breath. I went from one problem to the next, to the next."

I had conflicting emotions about Mom. Yet, I felt sorry for her. Certainly, I had compassion for her. I understood that my mother felt lost after the death of my father and, given the pain and turmoil of her last two relationships, I also believed that she must have had unresolved issues in her life. In the subsequent years, many people asked me about my mother. "What was her childhood like? What happened to her that caused her reactions to life and to you?" To this day I am not privy to those answers. I'm not certain that even Mom is aware of the traumas that defined her life.

Although Mom didn't accept responsibility for her choices, to my amazement, she did examine her failures verbally. I hoped she was coming to terms with her "mistakes" and that there was a promise for a "real" relationship with my mother.

* * * * *

Boundary issues are common in abusive family systems. Abuse victims and survivors are often compelled to empathize with those who harm us. Other individuals also insist we should have compassion for an offender in an effort to resolve conflict. I failed to realize that having compassion for another person is not a license to allow mistreatment. Compassion should go hand-in-hand with clear, respectful boundaries. Again, *feeling* compassion didn't mean I had to *act* on compassion and put myself in harms way.

Within a year of Mom's visit, my husband and I decided to return to Washington with our daughter, Tara. My excitement brimmed over with the uncontained anticipation of reconnecting with my mother. Yet it took but an instant to dash my hopes and expectations. Mom didn't want to see me. The change in her demeanor since she had come to visit me in California devastated me. Mom tried to come to terms with her marriages by blaming me for her choices.

"I resent the things you have done," she lashed out. "When you were only twelve years old, you made my decisions for me and made me stay married to Ed. We could have been rid of him, but because of you, I stayed married to him years longer than I should have!"

The delusion and mixed signals made my head spin. Mom's tight, angry voice cut through me as she provided a laundry list of my character defects and the ways in which I had made her life a living hell. She said she didn't like me. She harangued me in an attempt to get me to admit that her misery was entirely my fault.

In my desperation for my mother's love and approval, I defended myself with headstrong passion. Consequently, we fought bitterly and I remained negatively tied to my mother.

Mom called Rob, and he attacked me as well for giving Mom a hard time. He screamed at me in exasperation, "Why can't you just get along with Mom?"

Full of pain and looking for understanding, I turned to my husband, family and friends. My pain deepened when everyone insisted that I must forgive, forget, and simply get along with my mother. I felt so abandoned, I didn't know where to turn.

I failed to individuate from my mother. I wasn't her equal. I was still a damaged child who felt responsible for her anger, blame, and hurt feelings. I couldn't separate from my mother, because unconsciously, I kept looking for the love and approval I never received as a child. Without thinking, I wanted Mom to replace the bad internal messages she had instilled within me with good internal messages. I wanted her to be my mom and finish what she started. I didn't yet realize that I could and should replace the negative messages myself. It would take many years and many failed attempts before I was able to learn to separate from my mother.

For women like me, who grew up with an erratic mother, security is a foreign concept.

Lucy Rose Fischer, Ph.D., in her book, *Linked Lives: Adult Daughters and Their Mothers*, writes: "For most daughters, it is the stability of the mother's attachment to them that allows them to go through the process of separation and develop a sense of independence."

Without the security of my mother's love, I responded to my sense of responsibility as I had in the past, by vacillating between rebellion and compliance. Either I rebelled against my mother with defensiveness, or I met her with peace-making endeavors.

Either way, I didn't make choices that benefited me as an individual, separate from my mother; therefore, I lived in emotional separation from myself.

Desperate for a relationship with my mother, I sacrificed my needs and succumbed to the pressure I received from family and friends to forgive and forget. At twenty-five years old, after living with the pain of constant chaos, I struggled to turn a blind eye to the abuse in the family and Mom's hypercritical nature towards me, all in an attempt to shed my scapegoat mantle, to "get along" and to feel loved. In an effort to buy Mom's love and that of my family, I read *Making Peace With Your Parents*, by Harold H. Bloomfield, M.D.

Naively, without requiring acknowledgment for my injuries, an apology for my suffering or any expectation for the end of abusive behaviors, I set out to "forgive and forget."

Despite following Dr. Bloomfield's insightful recommendations to a T, peace was not on the horizon. Succumbing to forced forgiveness inadvertently put my healing on hold. I actually betrayed myself when I accepted betrayal as part of my relationship with my mother.

CHAPTER THREE

Scapegoat Mantle

Brandon was six years old when Mom married again. Her fourth husband, Lou, was another alcoholic. He mistreated my little brother, interfered with my own children by undermining my parenting, and alarmed me with the constant presence of firearms. He had guns and weapons everywhere throughout Mom's house.

When my daughters were four and six years old, we attended a family gathering at Mom's house. Upon entering another room to check on the kids, I was horrified to find a gun lying on the table where they were playing "Go Fish." I quickly went to check the weapon. It was loaded. I was furious! The children were playing at a table with a loaded gun.

Whenever I brought these issues to Mom, she "blew them off" or became angry and questioned, "Why do I always have these problems with you and never the boys?"

Each time I heard these words, primal fear gripped me, turning my emotions to slush. As is common with children of abuse, my growing brain wired itself in response to my trauma. Long into adulthood, we all continue to respond to our circumstances in the way our brains have been programmed. My brothers and I each survived our lives and abuse based on our family roles. Rob was Mom's protector. He clung to the only thing he had to hold on to—Mom—

and placed his blind loyalty with her. Rob acted out the violence he experienced and accepted any amount of abuse. He went to any length necessary to insulate Mom emotionally. Randy's role was to become the invisible one. He was sweet and agreeable, blending into any situation with his people-pleasing skills. I was the troublemaker when I fought against our abuse and my role as the family scapegoat. In other words, as a matter of survival, Rob fought *for* "status quo," I fought *against* "status quo" and Randy flowed whichever way the wind blew.

Research affirms that when we are children, our developing minds are programmed both psychologically and physically. In a December 14, 2000 press release titled "McLean Researchers Document Brain Damage Linked to Child Abuse and Neglect" (http://www.mclean.harvard. edu/news/press/archived/20001214_child_abuse.php), researchers at McLean Hospital, a Harvard Medical School affiliate, released their findings on the effect child abuse and neglect can have on brain structure and function.

According to Martin Teicher, M.D., Ph.D., director of the Developmental Biopsychiatry Research Program at McLean, "A child's interactions with the outside environment causes connections to form between brain cells. Then these connections are pruned during puberty and adulthood. So whatever a child experiences, for good or bad, helps determine how his brain is wired."

He also reports that, "This is not something people can just get over and get on with their lives."

My own brain became wired to respond to scapegoating with unmanageable anxiety.

In the McLean Study, Teicher also states: "We know that an animal exposed to stress and neglect early in life develops a brain that is wired to experience fear, anxiety and stress. We think the same is true of people."

In many ways, I was emotionally dependant upon my family. When I felt blamed, I freaked out and looked to them for help, love, and approval. They then blamed me again! Now I felt a sense of primal desperation that needed immediate attention and resolve! However, I didn't know how to quiet my distress or break free from my pattern. The scapegoat/troublemaker role hung over me like a dark cloud. This role was an integral part of my being and colored all my interactions with my family.

As an example of the crazy-making conversations in which I continually engaged in with my family, I'll offer the following more in-depth illustration:

A few years after Randy moved to California, we all went to visit him. I stayed in California for a few days and was the first to leave after our visit. Mom, Lou and Brandon stayed on for several more days. Rob stayed even longer.

Randy called a couple of weeks later to tell me he was quite upset with me. "I'm mad at you for what you've done to my relationships with the family," he stated in an accusing tone.

"What are you talking about?" I questioned.

"I moved to California, Nancy, because of you and all of the rotten things you have said about this family," he continued. "You had me convinced that they are all terrible. But they're not. I had a great time with everyone during our visit. Mom and Lou were great to me. Rob stayed after everyone left and we talked all week. We have a great family that wants to be close, and you scared me away."

Primal fear seized me instantaneously and yet I didn't know how to release myself from the grip of constant blame. "Randy, I'm glad you had a good time with the family," was all I managed to interject.

"Rob and I talked," he went on, "and I'm moving back to Seattle to work for him on his tool invention."

"I think that's great, Randy."

"But this time, I'm not going to let you tell me that the family is terrible, cause they're not," he declared. "Rob and I haven't gotten along all these years because you told me he was mean to me."

I was shocked. "What are you talking about?" I questioned again.

Randy's explanation was that when Rob asked him to move back and work with him, he told Rob that he was reluctant because he never felt like he had his respect; that Rob always acted like his father, bullying and teasing him.

Randy went on to say that Rob informed him, "That's not true! Nancy told you that stuff! She's made you believe that I was mean to you, but I wasn't."

Randy persisted, "I reminded Rob about the time Mom and I moved back home after she divorced Bill. He didn't like the way I was treating Mom. While I was in her room, talking on the phone, Rob barged through the door, hung up the phone, threw me on the bed and started screaming at me. Well, Rob told me that that isn't how it happened at all. He said that you made me believe it happened that way."

My anxiety rose to an alarming crescendo! All of the muscles in my body tightened and my breathing became quick and shallow. Before I knew it, I jumped back into my end of the scapegoat role with full-blown desperation and defensiveness. "Oh my goodness, Randy," I responded in horror. "I don't believe this. The memories you have of the family and of Rob are your own. I have never heard that story let alone "planted" it in you. I was living in California during that period. Further, if you want to take a look at your childhood and family relationships, I think that's great and I wish you all the luck in the world. But I'm not going to be there for you. When Mom wanted to look at her relationships with Ed and Bill, she made peace with herself by blaming me. Then when Mom and I didn't get along, Rob protected Mom by blaming me. Now you and Rob are trying to figure out why you don't get along, so once again you can all just sit back and blame me. 'It's all Nancy's fault we don't get along. Yeah, we're okay.' Well, I call that 'bullshit.' You can deal with your relationships on your own. I'm no longer available as family scapegoat. I do love you, Randy, and I'm sorry for your pain. But I can't help you."

I spent the evening "worked up." I paced back and forth across the room, obsessively running our conversation through my head—arguing, defending, restless and agitated.

Of course, I was still available as the family scapegoat as long as I was enmeshed with my family and continued to play my role. When we are enmeshed with our families, we lack the boundaries necessary to distinguish between our own feelings, needs, and priorities, and those of our family members.

It would take stepping outside the abusive family system much later, and years of deconstructing the way my growing brain had been constructed, before I could successfully "re-wire" my psyche and put down my scapegoat mantle.

Ultimately we know deeply that the other side
of every fear is a freedom.
—Marilyn Ferguson

Randy did return to Washington. He and Rob fought viciously as they tried to work together. Disillusioned about the family, Randy returned to California. Before he left, he relayed to me the difficulties he had with the family. He offered a list of ways in which Mom and Lou treated him like a child. "And," he continued, "Lou is out of control. Once, during a visit to Mom's, Lou shot off a rifle right within the city limits at some birds flying over the house. He was drunk and said the chirping was driving him crazy. When the neighbors came over to say they heard gunshot, Lou told them I had set off a firecracker."

"Oh my goodness, Randy," I said, astounded. "Does Mom know this?"

"Yes. She says it won't happen again. Brandon also told me that Lou got drunk and made him drive him to a recycling station. Can you believe that?" He continued, "Eleven years old and he's out driving for miles on the city streets. Brandon said he was scared to death."

"Randy, something has to be done!" I said in earnest. "We have to talk to Mom."

"No, don't talk to Mom," Randy warned, "She already knows and she said it won't happen again. Just let it be."

Any time I gingerly pointed out Lou's antics, abusive behavior and my concern for Brandon, Mom guarded her marriage by becoming angry and scolded me to "get along with Lou." If I pressed further, Mom called me horrible names and phoned the family to tell them I was irrational. Family members in turn admonished me to stop causing trouble.

The loneliness I felt was crippling. After reaching a point of desperation, I sought out therapy, hoping to resolve my anguish. Over a period of years, my relationship with my husband deteriorated to the point of no return. After much hard work in individual and couples counseling, I made the painful decision to end my marriage.

* * * * *

My mother's marriage to Lou came to a climactic conclusion when drunk, cursing, and bumping around the house, he discharged a gun in Mom's direction. Mom called the police; her fourth marriage ended; and she fled to my house for the night. The next day, Mom asked me to take her home and stand by while Lou finished packing. We waited anxiously in the living room while Lou finished with his task and left without incident.

Mom ran out to the street and took a picture of Lou as he drove away. "I'm going to take this picture and mount it next to the bullet hole in the wall," Mom declared. "The next time a man looks even remotely interesting to me, I'll look at that bullet hole and this snapshot to remind myself how much I don't need a man in my life."

We sat and talked for a while before I left. Mom told me the same thing she told me after she left Bill, "Why didn't you do something to prevent me from doing this? If I become involved with another maniac, stop me. Do whatever it takes to make me see reason," she demanded.

During her last three relationships, Mom had gone to cruel lengths to insist that I accept the abusiveness of her partners and blamed me for making trouble. Yet at the end of each relationship, she said, "Why didn't you stop me?"

In my compliance and "forgiveness," I swallowed my bitterness. I allowed my mother her delusion, while my resentment burned inside me.

CHAPTER FOUR

Pinning My Hopes on Me

When I was thirty-two years of age, Mom surprised my brothers and me with Christmas letters. The moving expression from her heart was the first "emotional" gift I recalled receiving from her and I cherished it. Mine said in part: "When I see you working at the cabin, it is 'déjà vu.' Your father had a lot of energy, and he really loved the lake and spending time there with his family. He would be very proud of his daughter and her family."

The letter touched me deeply. Mom's uncharacteristic sentiments left me craving for more.

The Lake was usually where we saw one another. After each of her marriages ended to Ed, Bill, and now Lou, I believed Mom was going to straighten out her life and our relationship would grow.

Mom and I visited often at my home or the Lake and we talked at length. She recognized that she had continually given up her life for her mates, and she felt bad that her children were the ones who paid for her mistakes. Mom relished in being able to relax, see people, and do what she wanted, when she wanted, without a man imposing thousands of rules over her and Brandon.

41

Mom extended herself to me in ways she never had before and she genuinely enjoyed parenting Brandon. Once again, I held out hope I'd have a mother.

During Mom's marriages to Bill and Lou, my brothers ignored the abuse and violence they dispensed. They became "good buddies" with her partners, enabling Mom to protect her relationships. On the other hand, I did not become a "good buddy" with her mates, but rather expressed disapproval of their abusive behaviors. While married, Mom deeply appreciated my brothers; however, when each relationship ended, she knew she had an ally in me and raced to receive validation for her decision to divorce. At the end of each marriage Mom and I became closer and she distanced herself from my brothers. Desperate for a relationship with my mother, I fell into this yet unrecognized pattern every time, only to find myself on the receiving end of her rage as soon as she recovered from the pain of divorce. I failed to realize that our newfound "togetherness" was only temporary, not the beginning of something new.

* * * * *

Before long, Mom had selected a new man. Smokey was cut from the same cloth as her previous mates. He was offensive in his manners; he "ran" the show; he overstepped his authority with my daughters and me; he was rude and crude; and, more than that, he abused thirteen-year-old Brandon. Within days of their dating, Mom gave Smokey a key to the house at the lake and he imposed outlandish rules, banishing my young brother outside the cabin.

Brandon called me nightly with tales of abuse and hurt feelings. Smokey never missed an opportunity to tell Brandon he didn't like him. He dictated constant discipline and chores, isolating Brandon in his room after finishing his tasks. Brandon lamented that he couldn't even sit in his room in peace. Smokey would walk into his room, shut off his radio, and leave. He often clipped Brandon in the head with the back of his hand as he walked past him and referred to him as "ass-hole" rather than calling him by name. The list of insults and abuses was endless. Brandon complained that Mom wouldn't intervene on his behalf. She either ignored him with deliberate silence, laughed off his protestations, or blamed Brandon. He pleaded with me for help and asked me why no one would come to his aid.

I felt horrible for my baby brother and angry that Mom continued to sacrifice the well-being of her children for the sake of a relationship with a man. Yet I didn't know what to do. Trying to intervene in the past had caused everyone to blame me for creating family problems, and nothing ever changed.

More than during any of her prior relationships, Mom's liaison with Smokey affected me with unmanageable anxiety. When she was married to Ed, I was still a child. As children, our young brains had not developed enough to take care of ourselves. We were dependent on the adults in our lives to teach us how to process the information we gathered from our experiences. As a child, I didn't have the ability to deal with my abuse—I dissociated from the pain. However, my trauma remained fused to me into adulthood. My pain resurfaced while watching in horror as yet another abusive man in Mom's life wreaked havoc in our midst.

I escaped to California during Mom's marriage to Bill. Free! Safe! A brand new start! Or so I thought.

During much of my mother's marriage to Lou, in an effort to buy Mom's love and that of my family, I succumbed to the pressure to "forgive and forget." I tried to ignore the abuse Lou dispensed—and Mom's betrayal, complicity, and her hypercritical nature—all in an attempt to "fit in" and to feel loved. It didn't work. And I felt guilty that in my complicity, I didn't protect Brandon.

By the time Mom had a relationship with Smokey, I was fed up! Fear for my youngest brother's well-being consumed my mind. In grappling with how to help Brandon, my old unacknowledged and unhealed wounds ripped wide open. Nothing I had tried in the past had worked. The family only turned on me, threatening me into silence.

Feeling helpless, hopeless and terribly frightened, my inner turmoil sent me reeling into therapy. Determined to end the cycle of violence in my life, I wanted to come to terms with my own abusive childhood and to learn new methods of dealing with my mother and the co-dependent structure of my family.

In the safety of therapy, I cautiously shared stories of Ed and the childhood violence that my family battered me for sharing before. All the while, I waited for my therapist to deliver the familiar crushing blow of blame. It didn't happen. My therapist responded with strength, and compassion, and he acknowledged the severity of my injuries. "Nancy, this isn't even normal child abuse. There are many well-intentioned parents who don't mean to abuse their children, but they do. Your abuse, on the other hand, was intentional. It was sadistic."

As my counselor validated my experiences, I became stronger and clearer about what had happened to me and the effect that it had on my life. He helped me begin the process of dissolving my isolation and moving forward.

I learned how to respond differently to my mother—to face her as an adult and to make choices based on what was best for me, rather than what was best for her by escaping, rebelling, or complying as I had during each of her prior relationships.

Unfortunately, the therapeutic healing process is very slow. It takes years to heal from trauma. Yet, I began the terrifying process of coming to terms with my mistreatment.

My family participated in what I would refer to in therapy as "island" thinking—thinking that only held true on the family island. When outsiders visited the "island," they acquired this thinking as well. However, once off the island, on the "mainland," these same individuals were appalled by abuse along with the rest of society.

Living amidst the denial of the family "island" for so long made it difficult to accept the reality of our abuse. Trying to forgive all these years caused me to suppress and downplay my anger and memories, because I couldn't forgive if I fully acknowledged my experiences.

Finally, I went to see Mom and firmly yet lovingly asked her to protect Brandon. "Mom, I love you, *and* it is time for the abuse to stop. I'm asking you to do for Brandon what you were unable to do for us. Protect him, Mom. Please protect him."

Characteristically, my mother was furious with me. She denied my accusations of abuse and reminded me once again that I was sick and the one with the real problem.

Mom called friends and family to tell them I was irrational.

Surprisingly, one by one, Grandma, Randy and other extended family members called me to ask my assessment of Smokey. Reluctant to reprise my old troublemaker role, I asked for their opinions first.

Everyone thought he was just awful. Their descriptions ranged from obnoxious, abusive, appalling, "he makes my skin crawl," and most often, "a jerk."

Smokey's presence in the family fold had a direct impact on everyone. Nobody wanted him in our lives and they all lamented it was unfair that he ruined our family gatherings. A number of family members told me that they refused to see Mom as long as Smokey was in tow.

For the first time, I had hopes of escaping my family scapegoat role. I took the opportunity to tell everyone how Smokey treated Brandon.

I had already stopped speaking to Mom after one of our recent telephone conversations. While listening patiently to another unbearable list of harsh criticisms about me as dictated to her by Smokey, my anxiety rose to a frightening boiling point. I attempted to quiet my nerves before responding to Mom. After calming down and gathering my thoughts, I called her back, "Mom, I called to tell you that I love you and I think we would get along a lot better without the criticism."

She hung up on me.

There was no need for me to go back for more. I couldn't "fix" my relationship with my mother. I had tried that in vain. At least for the present, I decided to distance myself from her.

Up until this point, Rob had not participated in the discussions concerning Smokey. During a phone call to Rob, I asked for his help in protecting Brandon.

"What do you mean? How dare you tell me Brandon is being abused?" he challenged, shouting across the wires.

"People have been chained and whipped since the beginning of time," he continued to rant and rave. "The human race has survived! We survived. He'll survive. I happen to be proud of myself and my family. You! You are sick and weak and unstable. You live in fantasy land. You always have and you always will." He hung up on me.

When Rob called each family member to tell them I was a "nut job," Randy informed him that Smokey did abuse young Brandon. "I've witnessed it my self," Randy assured him. Then he requested Rob's help with a solution to the "Smokey problem."

Once again, my grandmother and brothers viewed Smokey as the sole detriment in our lives. I viewed the abusive family system we all functioned within as the problem. Yet I didn't know how to affect a change.

When most family members refused to see Smokey, Mom told Brandon that the family would no longer be able to have get-togethers.

Brandon called each family member, quite upset. "Why can't this family get along? Why won't anyone come over anymore? I don't get to see anyone."

As everyone plotted ways to "get rid of Smokey," I advocated for a family intervention with Mom. Nobody wanted to speak to her directly. They didn't want me to either. Against the protestations of my siblings, I spoke with Mom again. Everyone was furious with me. The family buzzed around like bees in a hornets' nest. Then I got stung!

The whole family felt the pressure Mom's lamentations had on Brandon, and they folded. Once again, I was to blame for everything.

Mom forbade Brandon to see me. In a last attempt to help him, I called Mom. Instead of coming to some sort of resolution for Brandon's sake, Mom ranted in a one-sided conversation about how I had single-handedly destroyed the family, that I was sick, a crybaby, and a crazy trouble-maker. She hung up on me.

After he talked to Mom, Rob called me to tell me he was furious with me for destroying the family. He screamed into the telephone receiver in what would be our final conversation, "You're not my sister anymore!"

Paralyzed by Mom and Rob's wholesale condemnation, my emotions shattered into countless painful splinters.

I was angry! Angry at myself! Why had I even tried to forgive my mother? I had been cheated, betrayed and ripped off! Here was my mother—four abusive relation-ships later—and she hadn't changed an iota! She hadn't said she was sorry, asked for forgiveness, or acknowledged my abuse or that of my brothers. Instead, she blamed me for making trouble!

With the help of therapy, I decided that in order to continue my recovery process, I would not be able to see Rob or Mom. At age thirty-five, in the summer of 1992, after a lifetime of severe physical and emotional abuse and betrayal, without malice and simply out of self-preserva-tion, I made the painful decision to "divorce" my mother. Since the age of eighteen, I had tried every available option to make my relationship with her work. It was necessary to cut ties with my mother, not because of the abuse I suffered as a child, but because of the life-long emotional abuse and rejection that I continued to suffer as an adult. At this point in life, my emotional survival hinged on not seeing my mother. To this day, I believe it was the healthiest possible choice for myself. The time had come to give up on the fantasy that my mother would love me and to pin my hopes on me.

Although I felt a great deal of sadness and loss, I realized that I needed to put my own family first. My sole focus shifted to providing a loving and protective environment for my daughters and me.

I called Randy to explain to him my decision to divorce myself from Mom. I assured Randy that I wanted him to make his own choices and all I wanted from him was a continued relationship. Much to my dismay, Randy simply walked out of my life. A short time later, my grandmother whom I loved dearly, became enraged and cut me out of her life for good.

Stunned and blind-sighted, I called upon all of my reserves to survive.

CHAPTER FIVE

Standing in the Truth

"Injustice anywhere is a threat to justice everywhere.
We are caught in an inescapable network of mutuality,
tied in a single garment of destiny.
Whatever affects one directly, affects all indirectly."
—Martin Luther King, Jr., Letter from
the Birmingham Jail, April 16, 1963

Breaking the cycle of abuse is one of the most important undertakings I have attempted in my lifetime. I knew that breaking the cycle would take more than not seeing my mother. Living a new life required healing, understanding my mother, our family dynamic and myself, if I wanted a better life for my children and me.

Long into adulthood, I was drawn to my mother, craving and searching for her love. Although rebellion was often my mainstay, on a certain level I accepted my mother's blame, denial and the minimization of my abuse. Yet, during therapy, I pondered how *I* would react if someone threw one of *my* children down a flight of cement stairs. The thought of anyone hurting one of my kids horrified me. How had my mother allowed this to happen to us? Although difficult, I began turning the corner from internalizing my mother's blame to accepting her responsibility for my abuse. This freed me from my denial. Once freed, I began to speak the truth and to realize that I was justifiably angry. I knew I *was* angry; but, for the first time, I gave myself permission to *be* angry. My anger helped me give voice to my experiences. Standing in the truth was a positive move towards breaking the cycle of abuse.

I suffered a huge price for standing in the truth. Taking a stand against abuse is not possible without breaking the silence and exposing injustice. Therein lies the biggest obstacle to creating an abuse-free family legacy.

Truth-telling is an uphill climb for the victim/survivor. In an abusive family, the rest of the family often condemns the family member who "breaks the silence" and tells the family secret.

Silence aids the abuser and shields him or her from accountability. Silence maintains "status quo" for the rest of the family. Silence is easy; silence requires no action. Breaking the silence, however, requires strength and unimaginable loss. I have since learned that an abuser will normally do everything within his or her power to keep the victim, survivor, professional, or other bystander silent. When the perpetrator fails to maintain silence, he or she will resort to discrediting the victim or bystander with persuasive arguments. Like many survivors, I found myself ostracized and alone. The spectators remained silent.

Judith Lewis Herman, M.D., describes this occurrence in her book, *Trauma and Recovery:*

> It is very tempting to take the side of the perpetrator. All the perpetrator asks is that the bystander do nothing. He appeals to the universal desire to see, hear, and speak no evil. The victim, on the contrary, asks the bystander to

share the burden of the pain. The victim demands action, engagement and remembering.

It is my experience that people don't want to believe the victim. There is something in us that wants to disassociate from the truth. We don't want to taint ourselves with the horrible acts committed by individuals that we care about in our families and our communities. Human nature is to deny the truth, protect our illusions and avoid unpleasantness.

Victims who try to break the cycle of violence by themselves usually face retaliation on top of abuse.

For twenty-five years, since the age of ten, I stood alone in the truth about the abuse in my family. In the years since the loss of my sacred childhood, I thought I was alone in this experience. Unfortunately, mine is not an isolated experience. There are thousands of survivors, such as myself, standing alone in the truth about our families.

The appearance of normalcy and safeguarding the family secret takes precedence over everything else. THE SECRET is more important than the victim. THE SECRET is more important than health, happiness, family or relationships.

Had I known the price I would pay, the losses I would incur, and the isolation I would feel for simply telling the truth, I would have thought twice. However, the truth always has a way of coming out—if not in this generation, in the next.

I didn't understand the power of THE SECRET. I wish I knew then that my resolve to speak the truth about my family would be tested time and again.

I loved my mother. I didn't want to hurt my mom, but I wanted her to love me too. I didn't know that when I told the big family secret, I would have to choose between my mother and the truth. Still I told the truth.

I worried that my family wouldn't love me if I broke my silence, but in the end, I didn't believe they would all abandon me either. I didn't know that one by one I'd have to choose between my three brothers, my grandmother and the truth. Still, I told the truth.

Life has a way of asking:

- Will you tell the truth even when the perpetrator retaliates?

- Will you continue to tell the truth even when the offender convinces family and friends that you are "crazy," that you lie, that the abuse is your fault, or that it is all in the past.

- Will you tell the truth when, one by one, family members and friends sever their relationships with you?

- Will you still stand in the truth when you find yourself standing alone?

CHAPTER SIX

The Triple Whammy: Abuse, Mother-loss, and Family Rejection

WHAM! It felt like a kick in the gut;
I could hardly catch my breath.
—the author

Initially, the separation from my mother brought relief. I rejoiced that I didn't have to suffer on-going abuse and emotional garbage. Nor would I have to endure the heavy load of constant blame and emotional rejection. Free from the anxiety of re-injury, my life improved immensely. When the celebration wore off, however, reality set in. My damaged psyche needed healing and attention; yet, I unexpectedly found myself all alone.

Naively, I didn't anticipate the crushing blow that followed my estrangement from my mother—the loss of the rest of my family of origin.

Through all the hurtful words, actions, deeds, anger and sadness, I experienced a huge void—a longing for the irreplaceable relationships that would be no more. No matter who was or wasn't to blame, my family was gone—and it hurt to my very core.

Whereas the adult part of me functioned proficiently, the frightened little girl in me cried out for a mommy. Suffering from the largest cumulative trauma of my life, now more than ever, I needed the mommy I never had—a mommy to help me cope with the absence of my mother.

I longed for my mom to do what she had never done before—to wrap her arms around me and tell me that everything would be okay, to say that she loved me and to acknowledge my abuse. Why couldn't she just apologize and fix this?

I had lived my life "on edge," worried that my mother, grandmother and brothers didn't love me just as I was, but rather only if I behaved just as they wanted me to. I was devastated that my fears were correct.

I became a numb, empty vessel. I quickly learned that divorcing a mother is a very unpopular choice in our culture. Wholesale judgments and harsh criticisms were my immediate penalty as I faced the world at large. "You only have one mother." "Some day you'll regret your decision." "Why can't you just forgive, forget, and accept your mother for who she is?"

Beverly Engel validates this experience in *Divorcing a Parent: Free Yourself from the Past and Live the Life You've Always Wanted:*

> Many of your family members and friends will simply not understand what you are doing…. Even if you feel you have to divorce a parent for your very survival, you may be criticized and judged harshly….These adult children are frequently judged and criticized by people who have

had totally different experiences growing up and who see them as simply ungrateful, selfish, stubborn, or lacking in respect.

Victoria Secunda further explains this occurrence in *When You and Your Mother Can't be Friends: Resolving the Most Complicated Relationship of Your Life:*

> In the family, the Bad Mommy Taboo is more heavily invoked with "divorcing" daughters than with sons. Sons who withdraw are more frequently exempt from family censure in a kind of automatic boys-will-be-boys forgiveness of—or at least grudging tolerance for—their defecting highjinks.

She goes on to say, "… many brothers have a hard time digesting a move as radical as a sister's divorcing her mother."

Most people try everything possible to avoid the pain of estrangement. I know I did. However, in retrospect, the estrangement from my mother was essential for healing; yet healing came with a price tag.

Having lost every relationship from my family of origin, I felt like the Universe kicked me in the gut and knocked the wind out of me. It took at least four years to regain my equilibrium.

In *Healing from Family Rifts: Ten Steps to Finding Peace After Being Cut off from a Family Member,* author Mark Sichel accurately describes the moment we become cut off from a family member: "… you know, for the moment, what hell is like."

* * * * *

As a single parent, there was nobody to catch me if I fell. The luxury of falling apart wasn't an option. I had kids to raise and a position to fulfill at work, so I inadvertently staved off authentic healing and mourning.

The reality of my family expulsion left me stunned. The shock, disbelief, profound loss, shame, and embarrassment were too much to bear. Trying to ignore the pain of family exile, I literally dissociated from my feelings and I "powered" through my life in silence. I didn't allow myself the normalcy of "feeling" life in the present, because my present life was beyond my tolerance for pain.

In a quick and matter-of-fact fashion, I implemented new family traditions for my children and myself. The prospect of starting over, all alone without any family, was very daunting. Occasionally, such as during the holidays, the dam of pain I held at bay cracked and the intense anguish momentarily seeped through until my mind once again banished my painful thoughts to a faraway place.

Just as with any "death," firsts were particularly difficult. First family vacations, birthdays, holidays—all the events that would be no more.

I didn't know how to deal with the loss of the Lake. The cabin was the only physical connection left of my father. My children had spent their weekends and summer vacations at Lake Roesiger, just as I had as a child and as my father had before me. Ill-equipped to deal with the enormity of this loss, I powered forward. We needed a new traditional get-away that would become special to my children and me. We chose the San Juan Islands as an annual destination and began building new memories even before we had the chance to mourn our history.

My mother's sister, Aunt Julie, invited us to her annual Christmas Eve celebrations, and we began the yearly tradition of inviting some old family friends, the Millers, for Thanksgiving and Christmas Day. For the first few years, I just went through the motions of doing something new. I dreaded the holidays and my heart was not in the task before me or with the people surrounding me. A number of years passed before I realized I had developed new holiday traditions that were more loving, fulfilling, and less stressful than any of my prior experiences. Once again, the holidays became a time of fun and excitement.

My friend, Nina, topped the list of a small circle of supportive and trusted confidants. I can't imagine what my journey would have looked like without her or my Aunt Julie. They stood by me during my struggle to rebuild holiday traditions, family traditions, and a new life for the girls and me without Mom, Rob, Randy, Brandon, or Grandma. Long before the estrangement from my family of origin, Aunt Julie had been an important presence in my life, offering the maternal and therapeutic guidance that was otherwise unavailable to me. Further, she lived an example of love, compassion and guidance as she navigated her own trials and tribulations with dignity and respect for others and for herself. Many of these traits had otherwise not been modeled for me.

After the painful moment in which my grandmother rejected me, I immediately called my Aunt Julie to ask if she was going to reject me as well. "Certainly not!" she reassured me. The courage it took her to make that stand would in the subsequent years cause undue pressure in her life. I am so thankful because her support was a salvation that made all the difference in my life between holding on or falling into the abyss.

I trust that what makes seemingly unbearable pain bearable is the ability of another individual to hold your pain. Nina and my aunt stood by me during my greatest times of need. Whether they consciously or unconsciously accepted this role in my life, they responded to the call! I will always be grateful.

Giving connects two people, the giver and the receiver, and this connection gives birth to a new sense of belonging.
—Deepak Chopra

I couldn't stave off mourning forever. Because speaking about the abuse had cost me my entire family of origin and resulted in the judgment of many bystanders, it would be many years before I summoned the courage to break my silence again. Finally, when the silent misery I lived with outweighed the risk of another wave of losses, I decided to speak out once more.

There is a need to speak the truth—to honor our pain and our losses so we don't remain "stuck"; it is important to move on with our lives. Our injuries must be brought into the light—acknowledged, examined and understood if we have any hope of healing, breaking old patterns and moving on to the life we deserve.

It was difficult for me to differentiate the trauma of my abuse with the trauma of estrangement. My abuse and alienation from the family were intertwined and I couldn't imagine that my family loved me.

Simultaneously, the time came to heal from my abuse, recover from the rejection of my entire birth family, and to deal with the "shame" of divorcing Mom. I realized that forced forgiveness didn't work for me.

Everything in my life seemed uncertain; yet, there was one thing I knew for sure—I no longer forgave my mother.

CHAPTER SEVEN

Saying Good-bye to Grandma

During my growing up years, Grandma had a positive impact on my life. She gave me what all children need—she
gave of herself. Quite simply, she spent time with me.
Grandma stated her affection with walks on the beach and
her almost eccentric, yet lovable curiosity with nature. She
spent time with my brothers and me, playing cards, cooking
us elaborate meals and spoiling us with treats. Grandma
shared her joy of crafts and cared for us when we were ill.
I cherished fond memories of my grandmother. How could
a loving grandmother reject her grandchild?

A few years after our estrangement, I wrote Grandma
that I loved her and wanted a relationship with her. She
never answered my note.

Six years into our estrangement, Grandma had a
stroke. Although Grandma refused to see me right up until her death, Aunt Julie called me when she slipped into
unconsciousness, offering me one last opportunity to say
good-bye. I left for the hospital immediately.

Sitting next to my grandmother's bed, I spoke with my
aunt quietly. Grandma lay still and never opened her eyes.

She did, however, cry out for "Mama" several times. "No matter how old we become," Aunt Julie commented, "we always want our mama."

My aunt left the room, allowing me a moment alone with Grandma. I sat with my grandmother for a while, just staring at her. The quiet moments with her were both sad and sweet. Warm memories flooded my mind, as I said hello and good-bye.

I held her hand and whispered, "Hi, Grandma; it's Nancy. I want you to know that no matter what happened between us, I love you. And I know that you love me too."

Even though her eyes remained closed and she lay still, she heard me. The tears that quietly streamed down her cheeks were her reply. I kissed her softly, said good-bye, and left her bedside.

My grandmother died not long afterwards.

My love and longing for my grandmother were central to me long before she died. Yet I didn't go to the funeral. The soul-crushing isolation caused by not attending her service left me devastated; however, I simply did not feel safe enough to be there. I'd "heard through the grapevine" that Rob wanted to hurt me. He had repeatedly blamed me for all our family problems. Grandma refused to see me even after my attempts at reconciliation. Mom told everyone that I had single-handedly destroyed the family. Randy blamed me for his decision to move away from the family, asked me to ignore the continued family violence, and abandoned me. Brandon blamed me in a letter, four years after Mom forbade him to see me, in which he said in part, "How do you get the nerve?... you tore our family apart…. I am reminded of the scars you have brought this family by your actions…. I once thought I would be able to forgive you for this, but now…"

The risk associated with attending the funeral and facing an angry wall of censure was too great. As long as my family misidentified the cause of our family fracture as my "illness," we were unable to mend the actual cause of our fracture. Without acknowledgment or a behavioral change, I didn't feel safe.

Attempting reconciliation with my family did not seem possible.

> *I cannot change other people; they walk their own path,*
> *And they live by what they perceive to be the truth.*
> *Only by changing my perception and awareness*
> *Can I change my circumstance.*
> —the author

For years, I had begged my family, especially my mother, to acknowledge my experiences and my role as scapegoat. I learned that I couldn't force other people to do their emotional work or to acknowledge my injuries and make amends. I could only focus on my own growth.

Mourning alone, I stayed home and wept all day. The rest of the family was together, mourning the loss of our grandmother and a segment of our history. Once again, I felt excluded and abandoned—all for simply telling the truth.

> *Although the world is full of suffering,*
> *It is also full of the overcoming of it.*
> —Helen Keller

CHAPTER EIGHT

Longing for a Mother's Love

For you created my inmost being;
You knit me together in my mother's womb.
—Psalm 139:13

The first time I read this beautiful verse in Psalm 139, I felt like an innocent child, discovering something simple, yet wonderful, for the very first time—like my hands or like my feet. Before anyone was aware of my existence, God chose me as His child and knit me together in my mother's womb.

This comforting verse brought healing tears to my eyes and restoration to my injured soul. Right from the beginning, I was loved; I was not alone.

My faith has carried me through some of my darkest moments.

In *Healing from Family Rifts: Ten Steps to Finding Peace After Being Cut off from a Family Member,* author Mark Sichel writes, "It became more and more clear to me that the answer to coping with a family estrangement lay much more in the realm of spirituality than in psychology."

Estrangement is an unnatural loss. Whereas death is "an act of God," estrangement is a rejection that feels like a personal statement of unworthiness.

Beverly Engels describes this bewildering sense in *Divorcing a Parent: Free Yourself from the Past and Live the Life You've Always Wanted* when she writes, "Losing a parent is devastating, even if you are the one who has ended the relationship. We feel abandoned even when we are the one who has left. How can one experience years of togetherness, however neurotic or abusive, and not feel the pain of parting?"

After her death, the essence of a loving mother always remains with her child. The child or adult child carries fond memories of a loving embrace, protection, comfort, safety and concern. When emotional hardships befall surviving offspring, they turn to the mother they carry within for self-soothing, for strength and for guidance.

The estranged child carries painful memories of their mother and of the rejection. When emotional hardships befall an estranged child, we often long for a mother's love. We search to fill the void created in our hearts by the lifelong emotional absence of our mother.

With death, we HAVE to accept the finality of our loss. With estrangement there is often hope of reconciliation—hope that the mother-love we have always sought will finally come our way.

When a mother dies, others acknowledge the loved one's loss with tenderness and compassion. But, when a mother and child become estranged, bystanders usually don't understand the dynamics of the separation. They often assume that the adult child is responsible for her own loss. I'm not sure how common it is for a mother physically or emotionally to reject a child; however, based on the large number of motherless women I have encountered, I would say that a mother rejecting a child is far more common than society would like to admit.

Because of the sanctity of motherhood, our culture does not recognize a "Mother Rejection Syndrome." There is little support and few resources for a rejected child.

In the anonymity of secret support groups many women grapple for answers to deal not only with a mother's rejection, but also with the added shame and isolation that results. The pain expressed by these women is truly heartbreaking. I can say without reservation that the pain of motherlessness is never fully extinguished. We find both sadness and solace that, in the presence of one another, we are not alone in this experience.

Estrangement is like the amputation of an intricate part of ourselves. It's a soul injury. We are alone in the world, floating like an untethered balloon in the wind— homesick, yet not able to find our home. My mother was the missing link in my life.

Each passage of my life brought forth new layers of mourning. I mourned all of the losses I endured long before my mother and I became physically estranged.

Witnessing positive mother-daughter relationships in others was especially sad. These mothers shared life's passages and passed on love and wisdom to their daughters. This was never so apparent to me as when a mother guides her daughter through pregnancy, and shares the joy of childbirth.

When a friend of mine had a baby, once again I grieved watching her receive incredible love and support from her mother. Witnessing such love touched me deeply—yet I quietly mourned for myself. I had been so alone when my children were born. How it could have been with my own mother there....

I traveled the road to womanhood alone, without my mother's guidance or example of what it meant to be a woman, a wife, and especially a mother.

My mother did not leave me a loving legacy or a blueprint to follow. Instead, she tormented me as I tried to navigate each unknown passage of my life and learned to blaze a healthy trail for myself and for my children.

My own daughters certainly illuminate my losses. Nothing can match the excitement of watching my children swim their first stroke or climb their first tree. I can still see Tara's eyes searching the auditorium for mine after she landed her first gymnastics competition, and Dawn's pride when she learned to jump rope for the very first time. Love matters. When it comes down to it, love is really all that matters.

Each time I celebrated my children's triumphs, I felt the impact of my abuse and of my mother's emotional absence in my childhood and youth. As I celebrated with my girls all the important passages of their lives—such as first prom, graduation and day-to-day success—I experienced both joy and sorrow. I felt delight and pride for my daughters, while I mourned that it took having children of my own to experience the pleasure and significance of these events.

It was also through motherhood that I experienced what it looks like to "hold" a child's pain. My heart breaks for my children when they experience hurt, disappointment, and loss, or when they disappoint me with poor choices. Yet, I celebrated that I had the opportunity to give my children the love, guidance, and protection that I didn't have. I rejoiced that all my hard work paid off, and I broke the cycle of abuse.

Today I am the proud matriarch of a new family legacy.

CHAPTER NINE

Learning to Mother Myself

Bitter are the tears of a child: Sweeten them.
Deep are the thoughts of a child: Quiet them.
Sharp is the grief of a child: Take it from him.
Soft is the heart of a child: Do not harden it.
—Pamela Glenconner

Here in the Pacific Northwest, one of my neighbors has a palm tree showcased in the front yard of their home. The tree is small in stature with drooping pale yellow-green palms. It appears out of place among the many tall and thriving evergreens native to the region. Often, when I drive by this little tree during hostile winter conditions, I wonder how it survives, blanketed in snow and ice. The palm knows nothing of dry soil or the warm climate of its native land. It doesn't know what it's missing—that there are more favorable conditions available in which to flourish. Like my neighbor's tree, I was unaware of the many loving conditions the human psyche requires in order to thrive.

The child in me sometimes still longed for a mommy. In the absence of proper nurturing, it is difficult for a

68

daughter to separate herself from her mother. I remained tied to my mother, needing the love and approval of the one person I was designed to pattern my life after. I needed a mom to say, "I love you and I have faith in you." I needed a mother to carry within me as a separate individual. I realized that mother had to be me.

I often read in books, and heard in therapy and from many individuals about the need to learn to "self parent." It was one thing to learn to parent my own children, it was quite another to learn to parent me. "How do I do that?" I asked repeatedly.

Nobody could give me a good answer. Finally, someone said to me, "There is no good answer, because the key to what you lacked from your mother as a child is locked within you; there is no universal template that fits for everyone."

Until successfully learning to self-parent, I remained bitter about the concept of internalizing my own mother. Becoming my own mother seemed like a poor substitute for someone cheated out of the real thing.

Like other motherless daughters, I longed for a mother to replace the love I missed. I thought only motherless people had to internalize a mother. I didn't realize that *all* adult children have an internal parent. Having an internal parent is what constitutes adulthood.

No parent can do a perfect job; therefore, every individual needs to learn to parent certain aspects of themselves. The difference for me was, whereas most people have much of their internal parent placed within them by the loving actions of their own parent, I needed to internalize a parent largely on my own.

It is difficult to identify exactly what one missed from a parent. How does one know what they have never experienced? A confusing aspect to self-parenting for me was that many of the qualities my mother deprived me of I gave to my own children without understanding I needed them as well. Many emotional "basics" did not seem obvious—like receiving physical comfort. Although my children were the recipients of my hugs, I didn't realize that because the child-me hadn't received physical comfort, my inner child hadn't internalized physical safety.

Hearing about a study made on prisoners who were never touched during incarceration unless they were touched violently made me realize that for the bulk of my childhood, this was also true for me. The little girl in me only knew violent touch! I needed to learn how to comfort myself.

Long into adulthood, recalling stories of family violence evoked powerful tremors in me. The muscles in my limbs quivered uncontrollably and no amount of effort could suppress the flood of shaking. I remembered the first time in childhood that my body shivered like a frightened animal, while anticipating the beating about to come my way. I should have had a parent to run to for a safe place to fall—for comfort and for protection. After each beating, I dealt with my injuries in isolation and on my own—without any soothing. I wasn't taught, nor did I learn to self-soothe. My "body memory" re-enacted these tremors any time I summoned recollections in my young life when I was at the mercy of those who tormented me.

As an adult, whenever my limbs shook uncontrollably, I began the ritual of wrapping my arms around myself and rocking in a rocking chair, providing myself with the physical comfort that I never experienced as a child.

The temptation was certainly present to have someone help comfort me; however, I knew that would defeat the purpose of this exercise. Ultimately, the "power" of a mother's love—the mother I was learning to internalize for myself—ended my shaking.

On many such occasions I visualized in my mind's eye the "child me"—the hurting, frightened, alone, and damaged me. These occasions caused feelings of sadness and compassion for the little girl of long ago—feelings that, although deeply mournful, were also compassionate, reassuring, and healing. I'd speak to the "child me" who longed for love and protection. "Talk to me, sweetie. I am here."

This brought me to emotional self-soothing. When a child is terrified, their pain can easily spin out of control. A caring parent teaches the child to modulate their pain by comforting them with love and assurance. In the safety of loving arms, a child learns to reign in their emotions. Through example, this mechanism becomes internalized in the child and they eventually learn to soothe themselves. Emotional self-soothing is another quality I lacked as a child and needed to learn to internalize for myself.

I also needed to internalize self-compassion. My mother taught me to place the needs of others first, rather than to have compassion for myself. I learned as a child that my pain was no big deal and that I should be considerate of other people's pain, but not of my own. While it is important to be considerate of others, consideration should not come at the expense of our own well-being.

Because as an abused child my perceptions were often blatantly denied, I needed to learn to stand firmly in my own reality, without permission from anyone else.

Although I argued that it wasn't "right" to burn my tender hands, or rub Rob's nose in spilled milk on the floor, or to otherwise beat and betray us, everyone I knew told me that my perceptions were wrong. Therefore, I constantly sought validation, trying to develop a frame of reference from others as to what was "right" and what was "wrong." What we learn as children follows us into adulthood. Even as an adult, those I turned to told me that there was nothing "wrong" with the way Mom, Lou and Smokey treated Brandon, nor was there anything "wrong" with the constant presence of Lou's firearms around my own children. Consequently, I had difficulty as an adult identifying what was and was not acceptable behavior. If I felt betrayed, and the "offender" defended himself or herself, although I argued that it wasn't "right" to betray me, deep down I questioned whether something was wrong with me, and I worried that it was indeed okay to betray me. I desperately searched for validation that I had a right to the way I felt.

Un-doing a life-long mechanism is very difficult to do. Needing permission to "feel" was so deeply ingrained in me, that even if I accidentally smashed my thumb with a hammer, I needed consent to accept my pain. In other words, if I was with someone who said, "Oh, it's no big deal," I'd either try to "power" through the pain, or I'd argue that the injury was indeed painful, focusing on the other person's perceptions of my experience rather than my own.

My pleas for permission to feel physical and emotional pain had left me stuck in one place. Without validation, I failed to resolve my pain and move forward. It seemed impossible to believe that my experiences and perceptions were valid when faced with denied perceptions. A strong internal parent was necessary to assure my inner child that I had a right to my hurt, anger, sadness, and fear, without arguing for that right.

During therapy, I literally needed to be taught self-compassion, self-soothing, and the validity of my perceptions in the same way a young child is taught. My therapist explained how to seek out people to receive validating and empathic responses until I could internalize them for myself, even in the face of denied perceptions.

Until people taught me what it felt like to be self-compassionate, I didn't know that a wide range of emotions existed for me. I needed to "unlearn" the way I learned to ignore my agony. Then I needed to re-learn a healthy method of expressing my sadness. It was very important for me to learn to cry for myself and to share those tears with others, which is no easy feat. Seeking empathic people required trust, and trust didn't come easily for me.

Trust is such a basic relationship necessity that if we can't trust a parent to love and protect us—whom *can* we trust? When we have been betrayed in our most basic human relationship—and that trust is never restored—how can we learn to trust ourselves enough to trust others? I learned to trust in baby steps—sitting with my emotions and letting my feelings guide me. I needed to feel the pain of misplaced trust in order to protect myself and seek out those with whom I could trust with my feelings. If we listen closely, pain is a useful resource for protecting ourselves.

* * * * *

One of the most difficult aspects of motherlessness is the sense of aloneness.

I keep my father's picture next to my bed. Sometimes, before lying down at night, I look into his eyes and remember how much he loved me. I carry my father's voice in me—the voice of the one who looked at me with adoring eyes and asked me child-like questions, the father who loved and protected me, who nurtured, hugged, and comforted me when I cried.

I thought about the love that I give my daughters and imagined myself loved in the same fashion.

I watched the way other mothers loved their children and imagined loving myself in the same way.

I thought about those in my life who do love me—my children, friends, and my partner.

I called upon my spirituality to internalize abundant love.

God provided me with healing tears to wash away my heartache. He sent people who were willing to bear witness to my pain. God blessed me with daughters of my own so that I could experience a loving mother-daughter bond.

Sometimes, in my darkest moments, I wrapped myself in a blanket and imagined God's unconditional love surrounding me like giant hands tenderly holding me, loving me and keeping me safe.

Slowly but surely, I worked through a list of emotional deficiencies that needed filling. This was a long, frustrating, and complicated process.

Many of the emotional necessities I lacked seem obvious to me now, but for many years, I stared right at concepts that I couldn't see. Even today, I find new ways to nurture myself.

I advocate for other abuse and estrangement survivors. Offering validation and empathic responses to other individuals is helpful for them, and it also reassures my inner child that I deserve the same empathy. This reinforces my new wiring as well.

* * * * *

I have heard that the relationship we have (or don't have) with our mothers defines all the other relationships in our lives.

Certainly, issues of trust, abandonment, and rejection manifested themselves in my relationships, often in the form of Post Traumatic Stress Disorder (PTSD). Whenever a terrifying flashback threatened my safety, I felt certain that the looming danger lay in the present.

During young adulthood, my PTSD episodes were extremely dramatic. They quite literally threw me back to the past—seeing before me people, places, and events from my childhood.

Although my children's father was a non-violent man who in no way resembled Ed, at times during our marriage, just like a veteran of war, I found myself on the battlefield of my childhood, seeing David as Ed before me about to unleash his fury.

These imaginary episodes were swift, violent, and ended as quickly as they started. They left me shaken and confused.

Prior to healing and understanding my patterns of behavior, a number of stressful or damaging relationships affected my life. These failures manifested themselves from my old programming—misplaced trust and inappropriate responses. I responded to feelings of betrayal out of fear, focusing on the other individual rather than resolutely safeguarding my own well-being.

After my estrangement from the family, my PTSD was more unnerving. It was harder to identify and it lasted longer. A puzzling aspect to these episodes was that I no longer saw the events from the past. The incidents were in the present; yet, I unknowingly *felt* the events from the past. This gave me confusing messages that were not easy to decipher.

Fortunately, my therapist diagnosed me with PTSD and I began the process of understanding how to cope with these episodes. My counselor told me that when we have an adult experience that unconsciously reminds us of a traumatic childhood event, we become "triggered" and terrified because of unresolved childhood feelings. This is very confusing because the "little one" in us (whose life did feel threatened) believes their survival is at stake, yet the adult is confused because they know that nothing is happening that will cause their demise. Therefore, in an intimate relationship, it sometimes felt like my survival was at stake, but I didn't know how to calm my nerves and "prevent my demise" because nothing in the present seemed to be a life-threatening event. My therapist told me that when I am terrified, I should place my feet firmly on the floor, take deep breaths and really "feel" the present, while calling on images of my father offering me comfort and safety. He said it is important to place new comforting visions on top of the old terrifying images—offering my inner child the safety she never received.

When confronted with hurt feelings, if my partner didn't understand my experience, like a woodpecker, I kept frantically requesting his understanding. My adult awareness was simply one of unknown desperation. Yet, unknowingly, the child-me relived the emotional circum-stances with my mother—literally believing my survival was at stake. Agitation eventually gave way to disasso-ciation, which never resolved the pain. After learning to recognize this desperation as PTSD, I'd say to him, "Oh, oh, I am experiencing PTSD! It feels like I am sinking in quicksand! Please lend me a hand because I don't think I can do this by myself. This is about me—not about you. It feels like my survival is at stake."

Then he was usually able to understand. If he still couldn't grasp what was happening to me, I walked away and calmed myself with nurturing images of my father comforting me. These pictures brought new comfort to old trauma.

Facing my fear of not being "seen" was the singlemost terrifying experience of my life, because not being seen during childhood threatened my very survival. If Mom had seen and protected me, I would not have been beaten, blamed or fearful of impending death. Therefore, I spent my childhood desperately seeking understanding, while programming my brain to put my safety in someone else's hands. I didn't learn to put my safety in my own hands, nor could I comprehend that I could protect myself.

My PTSD also presented itself in the presence of anyone who seemed to have a matriarchal role in my life. A few years ago, I went on a four-day women's retreat with my aunt and my two daughters. The last night I went to bed feeling "on edge," experiencing that familiar sense of "impending doom," as if my world were coming to an end. Shaken by the unknown cause of my fear, I hoped the morning would magically bring solace.

The disappointment of waking up still terrified brought the realization that I was experiencing PTSD. But why?

As we arrived home later that day, I realized that the extended time spent with my aunt precipitated my PTSD.

Unconsciously, fear of another family rejection threatened my inner-child's sanity and survival. However, the adult in me struggled with confusing, unknown fear.

My aunt had steadfastly stood by me during years of family estrangement. She was kind, generous, and loving. It didn't make sense to me that the world as I knew it now seemed to be coming to an end. It became obvious to me later that this had nothing to do with my aunt or the present; this was about my mother and the past.

For the most part, I did come to terms with my Post Traumatic Stress Disorder. Occasionally, my mind still convinces me that an unimaginable disaster looms just around the corner. I can spend days living "on edge" with feelings of unknown impending doom until I "shake myself" and remember that my fear is just my companion PTSD. This realization calms my nerves and reminds me that my fear is in the past and that I am safe in the present.

* * * * *

The Ipce, a forum for scholarly discussion about the understanding of mutual relationships between children and adults, states in an article titled, "Environmental Influences on Brain Development" http://www.ipce.info/library_3/files/glaser/glaser_2.htm:

> The process of neural plasticity in response to learning and the acquisition of new memories continues throughout childhood and into adulthood. Although the processes of plasticity enable the brain's structure and function to continue to be modulated in response to environmental input and the organism's needs, there is evidence that plasticity in the adult brain is limited.

In other words, re-wiring the way our brains are constructed by our childhood experiences is a difficult task, but it can be done.

When my children were little, we had a large cedar tree in the back yard that became caught in a wire fence. After removing the deeply embedded wire from the cedar, the tree continued to grow. Once the tree became large enough that it threatened our house, we cut it down in segments. While examining each section, we could see the perfectly round growth rings in the portion from the base of the trunk; however, the section caught in the fence had a disturbing pattern of contorted growth rings. In time, the tree re-grew normally above the area where we removed the fence. That odd shaped pattern in the tree remained a part of its wiring, but it did heal. Of course, the longer the fence stayed in the tree, the longer it wired itself "wrong" and the harder it was for it to set itself "right" again. The same was true for me. I began placing new wiring on top of the old. Sometimes it still seems natural to go back to the "old" wiring. Then I remind myself to strengthen new healthy messages, feelings, and responses.

For me, one of the most difficult patterns to break was that of my role as a scapegoat.

During my years of family exile, I often heard second-hand information from mutual family friends and acquaintances concerning my responsibility regarding the family fracture and my estrangement from my mother.

People often asked, "Why won't you see your brothers?" "What's past is past." "I don't understand why you don't get along with your mother. She seems nice to me."

The scapegoat in me was horrified. The weight of thirty years of blame crashed down on my psyche. Feelings of primal fear, anxiety, and stress flashed to the surface as I ran a list of indignant defenses through my head.

In the early stages of my recovery, I responded the way I learned in childhood. Sometimes I retreated into painful silence, allowing the agonizing words to torture my soul. Other times, I defended myself hoping for validation and acceptance. Either way, my responses did nothing to quiet my deep sense of blame and feeling misunderstood.

As time marched on, with the help of others, I learned to put down my scapegoat mantle. They say time heals all wounds. Yet, it is not the mere passage of time that heals—it is what we do with that time.

With experience, I learned initially to only share my trauma with people who already supported me. They helped me replace the majority voice I heard, from that of abuse and blame, to that of love. They provided me with the confidence necessary to heal and move on with my life.

With the support of trusted individuals who helped set a foundation of validation and acceptance, I stood firmly in my own experience even when faced with those who didn't understand.

Randy and I shared a mutual friend since we were toddlers. Chris had a heart as big as the whole of humanity. He liked everyone and everyone liked him.

Chris struggled with our family estrangement; however, I never discussed my family with him in order to honor his relationships with my family members and to keep him out of the middle.

One day, Chris told another mutual friend of ours, "I don't understand why Nancy won't see her family! She has a great family. Why can't she just let go of the past? I really wish she would have a relationship with Randy." He went on to provide persuasive arguments for my culpability over the brokenness of our family.

Listening to the story angered me. My old wiring sent me down the path of stress, anxiety, and desperation. Though it had been many years since I had seen my family, even apart from them I couldn't escape my scapegoat status.

Fortunately, I remembered not to fall back on old patterns and instead to strengthen new wiring. My circle of support allowed new loving voices to drown out old blaming, angry voices.

Rather than retreating into silence, or reciting a list of defenses, I called Chris and told him what I had heard. To his credit, Chris immediately confessed, "I'm sorry, Nance. I shouldn't have done that. I care about you guys and it is sad for me that you don't have a relationship with Randy. I feel like I am in the middle."

I said to my friend, "You know, Chris, I love you, and I know that you love Randy."

"I love you too," he said softly.

"I know," I continued. "And, you have a great relationship with Randy. I don't want to change that; I'm glad you have each other. However, the situation between Randy and me *is* between Randy and me and frankly, what happened between us isn't any of your business. I know that you feel like you are in the middle and you want us to reconcile. However, you don't know what really happened and I'm not going to discuss it with you. I want you to just accept and respect my decision. So in the future, please let it alone."

As uncomfortable as it was to call Chris, I stood tall—my tenure as the family scapegoat was coming to an end.

Chris promised me that he would no longer interfere in my relationship with Randy and he made good on his oath. I'm sure keeping quiet was difficult for Chris and I am grateful to him. In order for him to keep his word, he needed to accomplish a difficult task—he put my needs ahead of his own.

> *A friend is one with whom you are comfortable,*
> *to whom you are loyal,*
> *through whom you are blessed,*
> *and for whom you are grateful.*
> —William Arthur Ward

Each day I journeyed further down the path of recovery, I discovered new ways in which my abuse affected my life, my relationships and my parenting.

Fortunately, the conscious effort to blaze a new, middle-of-the-road trail for parenting my children heightened my awareness as a mother. Through classes, books, consulting with professionals, and modeling successful parents, I endeavored to hold onto the good my mother provided me in childhood and replace the bad. Hopeful that my children wouldn't suffer as I had suffered, I made a conscious decision to listen to, care for, and "see" my children. Walking the fine line between the conscious choice not to be my mother and the less conscious choice not to be her polar opposite, kept me on my toes.

After my children reached adulthood, much to my dismay, I realized I had leaned closer to "opposite" from my mother and had become overly involved in my children's lives. Fortunately, they were good about letting me know

I needed to "back off," and I did (okay—I did for the most part).

Children often repeat modeled behavior, both good and bad, passed down through the generations. They learn how to respond to their environment and relationships based on what we teach them. Unfortunately, I modeled for my children certain behaviors and responses in my adult relationships that resulted from my old wiring and abuse. Therefore, my children developed some typical "abuse responses" in their relationships without experiencing the abuse themselves.

Whenever I discover new ways in which my abuse affects my parenting, I tell my children what I have done, apologize, and make a sincere effort to change my behavior.

Today, I'm no longer bitter about the necessity to internalize a mother, but rather, I bask in the security of having an internal mother who helps provide my own safety and well-being.

A VISIT WITH ME
By Jan Kolb

I wish that I could go to be
With that little girl in me.
Returning then to her birthplace
I would greet her with embrace.
How good to see that little child—
Always shy and very mild.

Today I find her melancholy—
Arm wrapped 'round her little dolly.
But she brightens as we talk—

With doll in coach we take a walk.
Dark curly hair and olive skin—
Ah yes—this little one's my kin.

Now Daddy says we'll go to shore,
We can hear the ocean roar!
He gives us now such sweet attention
Holds our hands—no apprehension.
Jumping waves we feel the spray—
Oh—we are at the beach today!

Now we three build castles there—
In the sun and salty air.
Tiny bathing shoes on feet—
Protect her from the burning heat.
Striped umbrella keeps the glare—
From Mother in her folding chair.

Turning back my calendar—
I have been again with her—
Doing things she loved to do—
When she was small—before she grew.
I long to wrap her in a shield
Before life's blows against her wield.

But she'll be brave as she can be—
And trust in God—because she's me.

Dedicated to: JGK
little Janice Elizabeth Gray   *May 3, 1991*

—Janice Gray Kolb, from *Cherishing: Poetry for Pilgrims*
Journeying On (Copyright © 2007 Janice Gray Kolb.
Used by permission of Blue Dolphin Publishing.)

CHAPTER TEN

Healing, Forgiving, and Overcoming Abuse

*The soul cannot forgive until it is restored to wholeness
and health. In the absence of love—how can one forgive?
With an abundance of love, starting with one's self,
forgiveness becomes a reasonable opportunity.*
—the author

At some point in every abuse survivor's healing journey, he or she must face the question of forgiveness. Are there some abuses too atrocious to forgive? Is it possible, or even healthy, to forgive someone who has never asked to be forgiven, someone who has never acknowledged any wrongdoing, and someone who continues to practice the same abusive behaviors?

I questioned how I could forgive my mother for a litany of unacknowledged emotional and physical abuses and betrayals.

Many survivors recovering from abuse—including physical, emotional, and sexual abuse as well as neglect, rejection, and abandonment—often wrestle with the conflicting senses of a longing to forgive versus not feeling forgiving. Many times, survivors feel a responsibility or a social pressure to forgive even when they have not healed sufficiently for that step to have an emotionally healthy outcome. All too often, well-intentioned friends and relatives ask individuals to forgive and forget. Survivors of family abuse often succumb to this pressure, and embark on a path of superficial forgiveness that does not honor the depth of the injury or enable authentic healing and forgiveness.

Any of us who have heard the words, "you have to forgive," knows that this added burden can actually impede our recovery.

Once I began to absorb the gravity of my abuse, the thought of forgiveness felt very unhealthy, like a form of denial that threatened my healing progress. When a survivor denies her feelings and sets aside her wounds, pain, anger, and grief in order to forgive, she often finds that she is not able to heal. Ultimately, in the absence of healing, forgiveness doesn't last. I have discovered that healing first is the basis for true forgiveness.

After realizing that forced forgiveness didn't work, it angered me anytime someone told me I had to forgive, because at this point in my recovery forgiveness wasn't possible. The Reverend Marie M. Fortune states in *Abuse and Religion: When Praying Isn't Enough:* "… healing must be carried out according to the victim's timetable."

After years of working on "forced" forgiveness while trying to maintain a relationship with my mother, the following years brought a "moratorium" on forgiveness. Initially, my pain was so deep that I didn't think I would ever be able to forgive. Nor did I intend too. Yet, setting forgiveness aside, at least temporarily, afforded me the opportunity to heal. The hiatus offered a valuable resource to validate my story with sympathetic listeners, to express my anger in appropriate ways, to mourn my losses, to protect myself, and to feel some sense of justice in the world.

I knew I stood on shaky societal ground when I professed, "I won't forgive!" However, self-protection and self-compassion prevailed and my journey towards healing began. The many years I spent loving and caring for myself planted the seed to grow enough love in my heart to love those who harmed me. For me, it was the courage not to forgive that finally liberated me from my abuse and set me free to forgive.

You will know that forgiveness has begun when you recall those who hurt you and feel the power to wish them well.
—Lewis Smedes

It can be difficult to find safe environments to have our injuries acknowledged, because people often don't understand the nature of abuse or the necessity to "divorce" a parent. Initially, I found my support in therapy and with a few trusted individuals. Like many of my fellow survivors, I avoided people who were not supportive and also topics of forgiveness, abuse, and estrangement that might result in harsh judgment and re-injury. The embarrassment and isolation of my predicament were painful until I became clearer about what happened to me and I was able to express myself with greater confidence and clarity. My circle of support grew larger until everyone I knew either supported me or at least accepted my stand.

In retrospect, the painful forgiveness process is clearer now than it was amidst the confusing detours, wrong-turns and dead-ends that I encountered along the way.

How then do we acknowledge our pain?

One way to acknowledge our pain is to receive emotional compensation and acknowledgment from our abusers. Our greatest opportunity for healing comes from the offender. When the person who harmed us is willing to offer restitution, we are truly blessed. This means the wrongdoer must be willing to acknowledge the harm they caused us, offer a genuine apology, demonstrate a willingness to restore what was taken, and change their abusive behavior. However, because of the chronic nature of abuse, most victims do not have their abuse acknowledged by the offender. When survivors do not receive acknowledgment from the person who harmed them, they need to have their abuse acknowledged by other individuals. It is extremely difficult to forgive something that, in the eyes of their families and communities, never happened. Support and validation offered from others dissolves our isolation and gives us the necessary strength to journey forward to the life we deserve.

Another way to acknowledge our pain and move toward the possibility of forgiveness is to feel as if justice has been served. This is an important part of the healing journey, and validation and acknowledgment are part of the justice-making process. Justice can be as limited as receiving support and validation, or as substantial as criminal prosecution.

In *Abuse and Religion*, Reverend Fortune also explains: "Once justice has been accomplished, even in a limited way, forgiveness becomes a viable opportunity. Prior to justice, forgiveness is an empty exercise."

Third, expressing anger is a necessary step toward authentic forgiveness. Once our stories are heard, the door opens to recognizing our anger. All too often, victims try to deny or suppress their anger, yet finding appropriate ways to express their painful experiences is necessary in order to heal. Survivors need to find safe methods and environments in which to discharge their repressed rage. Discharging anger frees the individual to honor her pain and mourn her substantial losses.

Forgiveness is not a single act or a solo act but rather takes place in layers, little by little, as other individuals—whether they are our abusers, our friends, our families, or our communities—are willing to share our burden of pain.

Finally, a victim of abuse must be free from abuse to acknowledge her pain and move toward forgiveness, and this often requires placing our trust in others to help us move away from abusive situations. An important and often overlooked aspect to healing is that of protecting others and ourselves from further harm. In order to heal, we must be free from the anxiety of re-injury. In other words, forgiveness is not possible if there is ongoing abuse, and in order to protect ourselves, we need the support of others.

It is easy to become impatient with trying to forgive because healing takes an exceptionally long time. After spending years receiving the validation I needed, I expressed my anger and grief and then I found myself starting all over again—each time at a deeper level.

This can feel like one is not making any progress; however, in retrospect I can see that each layer of recovery was dependant on my prior healing experiences.

At first, I simply acknowledged and understood how I was abused. Once I worked through this level of healing and lived with it for a while, I discovered numerous ways

my abuse damaged me and I had to go through the validation, anger and mourning process all over again. I repeated
these healing steps when I discovered how my abuse affected my adult relationships, and then again, when I
realized I needed to heal my relationships and myself by
replacing old unhealthy internal messages, feelings, and
responses with new healthy internal messages, feelings,
and responses.

Healing requires a great deal of time, self-examina-
tion, hard work, and pain. Yet once an adequate amount
of healing has been accomplished, forgiveness becomes a
viable opportunity. Forgiveness doesn't mean that we "ex-
cuse" offensive behavior; it doesn't mean forgetting or even
trusting the person who harmed us. Nor does it require us
to "let go" of our safety. Rather, forgiveness means to let go
of resentment and find peace. For me, healing sufficiently
to even entertain the possibility of forgiving my mother,
required many years of hard work. I made great strides
toward forgiveness when I realized that I didn't have to
trust my mother enough to resume a relationship with her
in order to forgive her.

In forgiving, people are not being asked to forget.
On the contrary, it is important to remember,
so that we should not let such atrocities happen again. For-
giveness does not mean condoning what has been done.
It means taking what happened seriously ...
drawing out the sting in the memory
that threatens our entire existence.
—Bishop Desmond Tutu

The mother-daughter bond is, I'm sure, the strongest of all human bonds. Although I was sad that it was not safe to have a relationship with my mother, I loved her. God knit me together in her womb. Sometimes I closed my eyes and visualized God tenderly embracing both my mother and me. I tapped into my own feelings of unconditional love for my children and I "borrowed" God's grace. Regardless of our actions, in the presence of unconditional love, for a moment I only felt the Lord's love for us both. And I felt peace.

CHAPTER ELEVEN

Accepting Estrangement

Accepting does not necessarily mean "liking," "enjoying,"
or "condoning." I can accept what is—
and be determined to evolve from there.
It is not acceptance but denial that leaves me stuck.
—Nathaniel Branden, American psychologist

No matter how much time passed, the estrangement between my mother, brothers and me seemed surreal. Aside from the effects of abuse in our lives, my brothers and I shared a tremendous amount of love. My early childhood with Rob and Randy bonded us in a loving history that seemed as if it should be impossible to destroy.

When we are cut off from our families, we are cut off from our "source." Author Mark Sichel explains it this way in *Healing From Family Rifts:* "We are affected by family in ways we can't begin to fathom because for so long 'family' was the only world we knew."

In other words, no matter the condition of our family soil, when we become cut off, our roots are severed from the garden of our origin.

Even after largely healing from my abuse, the pain of separation seemed to linger. Although the agony of estrangement lessens with time, many people are disheartened when the void created by the absence of their families continues to rear its heartbreaking head. We wake up each morning to the continued rejection and we must somehow learn to live with the pain.

An effective means of lessening the pain of separation is networking with other individuals who are cut off from family members. We find that we are not alone, that we have endured the same agonizing experiences and ramifications. Our shared experiences help to ease our pain and aid in finding solutions for common ailments.

It is comforting to share information concerning methods we have implemented to navigate similar circumstances. A common concern for parents with young children is to worry about the effect estrangement will have on their kids. Most adult children I know who have severed their relationship with a parent have done so as a result of abuse.

Many adult children are clear—certainly those who have experienced sexual abuse—that they don't want their own children left unattended with their parents. Yet, they often find themselves legally or emotionally embattled with their parents over visitation with their children.

Other families walk the fine line between wanting their children to receive the good their families have to offer, while guarding against harmful circumstances. Unfortunately, many of these families often find their children "in the middle," receiving confusing messages from both sides as to who was right, who was wrong and who is to blame for the estrangement.

Although my children are now grown, Tara and Dawn were thirteen and ten when we became cut off from my family. They felt hurt and rejected. Tara and Brandon were only one year apart in age and were particularly close. She regarded him as a brother. Suddenly to lose her tender-hearted "brother" amounted to a devastating loss. Because my mother forbade Brandon to come to our house, Tara asked if she could visit Brandon at my mother's house. I felt torn. Like many of my estranged counterparts, I worried about her safety as well as feeling concerned that my mother may attempt to turn Tara against me in an effort to perpetuate the same old myth of a close loving family—destroyed by an unbalanced daughter. Yet, I loved Tara and I didn't want her to lose this important relationship. I told her she could go to her grandmother's house.

Tara ran for the phone to ask her grandmother if she could come for a visit. My mother told her, "No," and blamed me.

Unlike my cut-off peers, who grapple with dilemmas over whether to allow their children contact with their grandparents, this was one aspect of estrangement I no longer had to endure. The cut-off from my mother and the rest of my family was quick, clean and absolute. Mom, Rob, Randy, and Grandma didn't show any interest in seeing my children or me again.

My grandmother had been more like a grandmother to my own children than my mother was. They were sad that she would no longer have any contact with us.

The girls loved their Uncle Randy. When he visited from California, he and his wife sometimes stayed with us and took the kids on fun outings to the zoo or ice-skating. Randy and Stacy took a keen interest in their nieces, involving themselves in their activities such as gymnastics or the "fad" of the day.

The girls were not close to their Uncle Rob. They hadn't spent much time with him; yet, they noticed his absence as well.

I thought about my family every day. I often wondered if they thought about me.

Eight years after my mother forbade Brandon to see me, I found an invitation to his wedding in my mailbox. Recalling my naive excitement after receiving a letter from Brandon four years earlier, only to be hurt by the angry contents of his note, gave me pause. Nonetheless, I regarded his invitation at face value, even though I didn't feel safe enough to attend the wedding.

I immediately sent Brandon and his fiancé a gift along with a letter revealing how honored I was to be invited to their wedding. I regarded their invitation as a wonderful gesture of love, wished Brandon and his bride-to-be every happiness, and expressed my desire to meet with them after the wedding.

Brandon is twenty years my junior and close in age to my daughters, Tara and Dawn. Growing up, Brandon shared our family vacations and spent weeks at a time at our house. He and my children played like siblings and our relationship was more that of mother and son than sister and brother.

Much to my delight, Brandon did call after he and his wife settled into their new life together.

With raw emotion, he expressed a great deal of pain over our years of estrangement. Brandon told me that to be fourteen and suddenly lose his family had left indelible scars. Although Brandon expressed a desire to reconnect, he also felt weighted in fear. "I'm afraid that if I become attached to you and the girls again, I'll get hurt if it doesn't work out."

I understood his fears; mine were much the same. Yet, I had only one concern, "There is the matter of the letter you sent me four years ago. I need to know if you still feel the same way."

Brandon cringed, "Oh—I'm sorry. That letter is one of the biggest regrets of my life."

That was all I needed to hear and we all began anew. We snow-skied, walked around Green Lake, played cards, shared some holiday/family gatherings and in general kept our time together fun and light. We avoided all topics concerning the family.

With longing and trepidation, we became reacquainted with Brandon and got to know his wife. Mares is family oriented and brought enthusiasm to many of our activities.

Hoping that my relationship with Brandon would deepen with time, I fantasized that our reconciliation would, in turn, lead to a reunion with Randy, and then possibly to even the rest of the family. My greatest fantasy was that Mom would finally accept responsibility and stop blaming me.

I dared not speak this fantasy aloud. Yet, Mom, Rob, Randy, and Brandon were in my daily prayers. I prayed for their well-being and that God would grant each of us the knowledge of His will in all matters concerning our lives.

Unfortunately, my superficial relationship with Brandon didn't succeed. Because we only scratched the surface without talking about anything of significance, we failed to bond. Although we didn't discuss our feelings on the matter at the time, I found out later that Brandon avoided talking about the family because he thought it would hurt me. He was right. Hearing about my exclusion from family events, only served to illuminate my pain and loss. Conversely, I didn't wish to run the risk of continued blame by sharing my hurt feelings. After all, this had resulted in my expulsion from the family to begin with.

After a few years of occasional get-togethers, Brandon moved, left no forwarding address, and simply disappeared from my life. What happened? Once again, my hurt feelings resurfaced. When it came to my family, rejection was a constant in my life.

A year passed before Brandon contacted me to tell me why he had stopped seeing me. "I had hoped we would become closer than we did and I felt as if I was betraying the family every time we got together." He continued with candor, "Every time I saw you, Mom called me for days raging about her 'side' of the story. It wore me down; it wasn't worth the grief in order to have a relationship with you. The 'pay-off' wasn't great enough."

As is common with estranged families, communication is fragile. I found out later that Brandon was trying to tell me *why* he had stopped seeing me, past tense, in an effort to start seeing me again. I thought he was merely offering me the courtesy of telling me why he was no longer seeing me, period.

Brandon also shared the family's "view" of me. He recited a list of the same old blaming stories I'd always heard about myself. I offered him a short synopsis of family history and concluded by saying, "What you are expressing to me, Brandon, is what I call "island" thinking. Island thinking is the kind of thinking that is exclusive to our "family island" and isn't found on the mainland. I don't live on the island anymore, so I suppose that is why we don't have a relationship."

Brandon and I parted, each believing the other had ended our involvement in one another's lives.

* * * * *

Ironically, when I was a teenager, my mother gave me some eerily poignant advice when she said, "In this world, twenty-five percent of people you meet are going to like you, twenty-five percent will not and fifty percent aren't going to care either way. Stick with those who like you and don't spend any time trying to influence those who don't."

As painful as our renewed cut-off was, my pain gave way to relief. It was time to give up on the fantasy of any possibility of future reconciliation with my family.

A difficult aspect to estrangement is the lingering hope of re-uniting. This new chapter in my life put my hopes to rest. Although I prayed for my family members every day, it was time to accept estrangement and learn to live with the reality of the gaping hole in my heart.

CHAPTER TWELVE

Mourning the Lake

After spending more than a decade cut-off from the family, life continued on as usual. My children were grown and I held a responsible position in a booming company that demanded much of my attention. In my free time, I seized every opportunity to avail myself of the abundant outdoor activities the Pacific Northwest had to offer. I spent time with friends, a new man in my life, and my adult children—hiking, camping, snow skiing, swimming, and boating on Lake Washington.

Occasionally, new hurts associated with my family cropped up and I found myself working through new layers of forgiveness. Fortunately, after laying a strong foundation for healing and forgiving, forgiving new layers of hurt came with less distress.

My healing foundation aided me in 2003, when I received a devastating blow. My mother had transferred the lake property to Rob, Randy, and Brandon—excluding me from my father's legacy.

When my father died, my mother, Rob, Randy, and I, each inherited our summer home on Lake Roesiger in four equal parts. Because my mother desired sole proprietorship of the property, she petitioned the courts for singular ownership and won.

Mom made a promise to Rob, Randy and me that she would transfer the property back to us in adulthood. When I discovered that she had not honored her promise and excluded me from my dad's bequest, my prior feelings of forgiveness gave way to anger. With a fresh wound, new healing steps were necessary before considering forgiveness again.

Forgiveness is a process, and anger is a normal, healthy, and necessary part of the healing journey. Although I was angry with my mother, I did not contact her. I had learned that any contact born of anger would not be healthy for either one of us. Although my mother had hurt me many times, I didn't want to hurt her or perpetuate our unhealthy relationship. Discharging my anger at her in person would not be helpful or appropriate.

A much healthier alternative was to express my anger in the company of safe and supportive individuals. Fortunately, I had developed a community of support, and I knew many individuals who were able to help me through this process. They helped me discharge my rage, and to let go of the circumstances that were painful to me. I gave myself permission to be constructively angry—to use my anger as an aid in moving past my feelings of betrayal. With creative enthusiasm, my partner Bill provided many ideas for releasing myself from the grip of this storm.

Different forms of anger exercises work for different people. For me, dark humor works like magic. Bill and I played "Hangman" with anti-mother phrases. When Mother's Day approached, Bill suggested that we make "Anti-Mother's Day" cards. We enlisted the help of many friends to come up with ideas for the cartoonishly violent greeting cards. We laughed for hours. The release I felt when we were done was overwhelming and my mother was not the direct recipient of my anger.

Once again, supportive individuals in my life helped to share my burden of pain. They acknowledged my injuries, helped me express my anger in appropriate ways, and stood by me while I mourned the loss of my father's legacy.

CHAPTER THIRTEEN

A Voice from the Past

During the evening of April 30, 2004—the anniversary of Dad's death—and twelve years since my brother Rob and I had last spoken, Rob called me at home. I didn't recognize the voice on the other end of the line even after he identified himself and asked the familiar question, "Do you know what today is?"

A short and clumsy conversation followed. I wondered why Rob called; he didn't really have anything to say. I had the impression that he wanted me to do all the talking. Finally, he said, "As the oldest, I thought I'd call and pass the olive branch."

I wondered aloud, "What does that look like to you?"

"It doesn't look like anything," Rob responded, "It just means that I passed the olive branch and now if you want, you can pass it back."

During an awkward silence, he blurted out, "Yep! I'm up here at this big, beautiful house on the lake!"

Momentarily, an internal flash of anger gripped me, then relief because I already knew about the transfer of the lake property. I had time to deal with the intensity of my emotions, before I spoke with Rob. Drawing in a deep breath, I pondered whether his statement was a cruel attempt to "rub in" my exclusion from Dad's legacy or an unbelievably clueless statement. I went with the latter.

I chose my words carefully, "You know, Rob, I'm sure you called as a gesture of love."

"I did, Nance," he said with sincerity.

"You are my brother and I love you," I continued choosing my words carefully. "I don't know that we can have a relationship without some sort of third-party intervention."

"I'm not saying I want a relationship," he retorted.

"Okay, well like I said, I regard this call as a gesture of love and I'm going to just leave it at that. Thanks for calling Rob, Good-bye."

Hanging up the phone, I re-ran our conversation in a repetitive loop. I was overwhelmed with conflicting emotions like the waves of the ocean being whipped by conflicting winds. I felt angry and, once again, I revisited my hurt feelings concerning the lake. I was simultaneously sad that Rob was not a part of my life, and grateful that underneath all the pain, my brother cared enough to call.

I often wondered if my family loved me. For many years, I was sure that they did not. However, after Brandon's attempted reconciliation and Rob's telephone call, I was sure that they did.

It appeared obvious to me that my family wanted to reunite, but they didn't know how to mend our brokenness. I assumed they wanted me to fix our shattered relationships and, although I knew what needed to be done, I couldn't change their perceptions or perform their emotional work for them.

A reconciliation with Rob required a significant change on both our parts. For my own protection, I needed to have my role as scapegoat acknowledged along with assurances that I would no longer endure statements of blame for everyone else's problems. I couldn't sign on for more abuse. As long as my brothers misidentified the cause of our family fracture as my "illness," we were unable to mend the actual cause of our fracture. As for my part, I wondered if I had healed sufficiently to respond differently to old family patterns. In the presence of a family member, would I still react out of desperate primal fear, stress, and anxiety, or had my years of emotional work and hard labor paid off?

I didn't believe that we could successfully navigate a lifetime of family patterns on our own.

CHAPTER FOURTEEN

Fear of Public Exposure

Within days of my telephone conversation with Rob, I received the unbelievable news that a publisher wanted to offer me a contract for my book, *Heal and Forgive: Forgiveness in the Face of Abuse*. After writing, polishing and pursuing publication on and off for more than a decade, I could hardly contain my initial excitement.

For twelve long years, with an uncompromising resolve to tell my story, I persevered through years of doubt and professional rejection.

Endeavoring to provide more than a simple re-telling of my experiences, the text placed the story within the wider framework of my search for healing and forgiveness. I prepared to present an unmistakable picture that would validate and provide other abuse victims with the information that eluded me for years. I shared my innermost thoughts, feelings and vulnerabilities in an effort to turn my negative experiences into a positive contribution to my fellow survivors.

With the reality of publication at hand, I felt nothing less than raw panic. To open myself up to public scrutiny took courage beyond anything I had encountered in the past. Setting out to tell the family secret—the secret that already cost me every relationship from my family of origin—could cost me even more. Concerns that my family would be hurt, angry, or even lash out, plagued me. Although I questioned the wisdom of taking such a risk—no matter the personal cost—I resolved to stand in the truth that no amount of punishment had been able to extinguish.

One confidante simply stated, "That takes a lot of courage."

"I don't feel courageous," was my weak reply. "I feel scared to death."

"It doesn't take courage if you are not afraid," she responded. "Courage is being scared to death and doing it anyway!"

Unable to quiet my fears—I consulted with a therapist and my minister concerning my worries for my mother. Accepting the possible repercussions publication could have for me was one thing; however, I wasn't comfortable with how this public exposure could affect my mother. My therapist and minister both assured me that my book provided my mother with a gift, should she decide to accept that gift. I hardly believed in the likelihood my mother would receive anything positive from this book; yet, I continued on my life's journey, making choices that benefited me as an individual separate from my family. I persevered, hoping my family would never discover the book was in print.

CHAPTER FIFTEEN

Unbelievable Turn of Events

To the outside world we all grow old.
But not to brothers and sisters.
We know each other as we always were.
We know each other's hearts. We share private family jokes.
We remember family feuds and secrets, family griefs and joys.
We live outside the touch of time.
—Clara Ortega

One evening in April 2006, while working at home before meeting with friends, I was surprised to find an e-mail from Randy in my inbox. He received my e-mail address from a mutual friend. Past experience told me to be wary of contact from my family and I wasn't sure what to expect in the contents of his letter.

Randy opened with a simple, yet delightful youthful memory and continued with questions about us. "I always wonder how you, Tara, and Dawn are doing," he wrote.

He also sent me a link to his family photo album. Suddenly, I found myself viewing pictures from the lives of family members I'd been excluded from for fourteen years. Randy had an eleven-year-old daughter and six-year-old twin sons. The photo album included pictures of Rob's children as well. From a distance, I caught up on the lives of family members I had either never met or no longer knew. Until that moment, I didn't know Rob's oldest daughter was married. She was a young girl when we stopped talking. Rob's son, whom I hadn't seen since he was preschool age, posed for the camera in his military uniform. Brandon and his wife apparently had two babies since last we spoke. It was emotional and peculiar viewing their lives. With the exception of my attempted reconciliation with Brandon and one phone call from Rob, I hadn't heard from my family or about them in fourteen years.

I viewed pictures of my family and yet, I didn't know them at all. Randy's photo album also incorporated many pictures of everyone enjoying the "family" summer home at the lake. It was both painful and curious viewing their lives.

I wasn't sure how to feel or how to respond. I had opened myself up with hope when Brandon contacted me only to feel rejected all over again. I was finally at a place where I accepted estrangement. Now what?

My old familiar "body tremors" waved throughout my limbs. After taking a deep breath and quieting my tremors, although I had a commitment with friends for the evening, I decided to stay home and sort out my feelings.

Randy's e-mail stirred up many overwhelming emotions. Slowly working through my feelings, I tried to process all the information available via the photo images. The snapshots evoked feelings in me ranging from hurt, sadness, confusion, anger, curiosity, warmth, jealousy, love, and many more.

Although I had many conflicting feelings, years of healing afforded me the ability to deal with my emotions.

Previously, I had longed for relationships with my family members and would have jumped at a chance for reconciliation. I dreamed that one day they would finally "get it," acknowledge what they had done to me, and lovingly accept me back into the family fold. Ironically, attempting reconciliation too soon, before adequately healing, would have left me more eager and less capable. However, now all the love, acceptance, acknowledgment, and help with healing I used to yearn for from them, I had received from other people and myself. I no longer knew my family, nor did I need their validation and help with healing. I only needed relationships that augmented my life. In an odd way, no longer needing my family left me in a stronger and healthier position to explore the possibility of reuniting with Randy.

My yearning to stay on a healthy course caused me to question the wisdom of my simultaneous desire to consider a relationship with my brother. I loved Randy and I believed he loved me too; however, in the past, love was not enough.

After attempting a failed "superficial" relationship with Brandon a few years earlier, I would only accept an authentic relationship with Randy. Many questions surfaced. Could Randy have a relationship with me independent from Mom? Could he accept me for myself? Would he still blame me? Had Randy experienced emotional growth as well? I wasn't willing to sacrifice my safety in order to have a relationship with anyone.

There is nothing like returning to a place that remains unchanged to find the ways in which you yourself have altered.
—Nelson Mandela, "A Long Walk to Freedom"

Taking the risk of another rejection concerned me. I decided to reply to Randy's e-mail by simply thanking him for the pictures and his kind thoughts. I also briefly outlined what the girls were doing with their lives and attached a few recent pictures.

After e-mailing Randy, panic got the best of me when I realized that my e-mail signature contained a link to the website for my book. Although I was shaken at the possibility of negative fall-out concerning this disclosure, supportive friends calmed my nerves and assured me I'd be able to handle anything that came my way.

After the initial shock, a huge weight lifted from my shoulders. If Randy knew about the book and still wanted a relationship with me, I knew he would accept me for who I am.

Another month passed before hearing from Randy again. I wasn't sure if he was upset with me after noticing the e-mail signature or if he missed the signature altogether and just hadn't gotten around to contacting me again.

Randy's second e-mail was lengthier than his first and every bit as genuine. He skillfully tested the waters by weaving together good memories from the past, information about the present, and curiosity about my daughters and me.

After writing Randy a quick note in response, an uneasy discomforting feeling settled in. Reconciliations require a significant change for both individuals. Even though I had completed a great deal of emotional work, I didn't know if Randy had accomplished any growth as well, or what his intentions were. Tara and Dawn expressed concerns about becoming re-attached to Uncle Randy only to lose him once more, especially after what happened with Brandon. Although I did trust myself enough to navigate my interactions with Randy, the reality was that we might still simply be unable to have a relationship. The girls and I contemplated the meaning behind his recent contact.

After fashioning a letter to Randy asking him point-blank if he wanted to reconcile, I set it aside, waiting for his next e-mail. Months passed without any more word from Randy, and I went on with my life.

In August of that year, I attended a family funeral. Having avoided all prior family weddings and funerals, my cousin lovingly extended his support to me and asked if I would attend his mother's service.

The funeral was a four-hour drive from my home. My partner, Bill, accompanied me for support. I'd be seeing my mother for the first time in fourteen years, and the event could be wrought with emotional pitfalls. Hopefully, I was up for the challenge.

We arrived just in time for the sweet and faithful service. After the ceremony, I said "hello" to some of my extended relatives and spoke briefly with each of my cousins before making a hasty retreat. I didn't have any contact with my mother or my brother, Rob, who attended as well. Mom didn't appear even to notice I was there.

A few days after the funeral, the mother of my oldest friend died in a horrible car accident. Mary and I had known each other since we were three years old, and her mother held a special place in my heart. While mourning and reflecting on the fragility of life, the precious time lost with my brothers weighed heavily on my mind.

I called Randy to ask if he was willing to talk to me. He said, "Of course. I e-mailed you didn't I?"

We talked for over two hours. Randy told me that he loved me, missed me, and had not known how to re-establish a relationship after fourteen years of separation.

He went on to say that when Mom transferred the cabin to my brothers, they gathered at the new house they built on the lake. They felt nostalgic about Dad and they missed me. That's when Rob decided to call me. Prior to this conversation with Randy, I had no idea why Rob had called.

Randy told me he had grown up and that he made his decisions independent from everyone else. However, he also said that he didn't want to tell Mom he was speaking with me until we had time to re-connect.

The spirit of our conversation was very loving and realistic on both our parts. Surprisingly, it was not awkward at all talking about my book or our estrangement. Randy surprised me with the words, "I'm proud of you for 'taking a stand,' healing and living a productive life in spite of the past."

When he asked if I would like him to read my book, I paused for a moment, "I'm not sure sure. You might not want to see me after reading the book."

"I think it would be helpful for me to read your book from the perspective of understanding your experience," came Randy's touching and surprising reply.

While hanging up the phone, the gamble associated with a "reunion" concerned me! However, my love for Randy outweighed the obvious risks.

* * * * *

A few days after my conversation with Randy, Brandon and I spoke. We discussed our prior failed attempt at reconciling and our hopes for a genuine relationship this time around. During our last effort at reuniting, we did not talk about the family. Avoiding family topics and genuine emotional issues caused uneasiness between us. For the first time, we had honest discussions about our feelings and our lives. Brandon also told me that he intended to read my book. In the meantime, I invited Brandon, his six-month pregnant wife and two children to meet Bill and me at an outdoor dinner theater on Labor Day weekend, for a performance of *Annie*.

There are many painful firsts when we become cut-off from our family members—first birthdays, holidays, successes, and tragedies—all dealt with alone. These same firsts can be bittersweet upon re-entry. Meeting my nephew and niece for the very first time touched my heart with smiles and tears—we had lost precious time, never to be replaced. Yet, Brandon's children were adorable, and the play mesmerized them with child-like wonder.

Randy flew to Seattle on business that September and stopped by my office on his way through. We greeted each other with a big hug, a smile, and a little re-acquaintance chatter. We toured my business and then sat down, caught up on our lives, and reminisced about old times. It seemed surreal to see Randy again; yet our visit felt relaxed, comfortable, and fun.

In December, during winter break, my daughter, Dawn, was getting married. I love her fiancé, Colin, and was excited about their upcoming union. Dawn, now an English teacher, and Colin were planning a large, yet meaningful wedding tailored to their own unique relationship. As to be expected, wedding preparations and all the accompanying stresses and excitement moved front and center in our lives. We were planning a wedding around the busy holiday season and adjusting to the overwhelming emotions surrounding possible reconciliations. Our movements with

Randy and Brandon were slow and tentative. Cautious optimism concerning my brothers hung in the air, while I waited for their reaction to my book. The prospect of reuniting seemed unbelievable after all these years.

Tara and Dawn were excited at the possibility of seeing Brandon and Randy again. A few weeks after we saw *Annie,* Brandon invited the girls, Colin, Bill, and me over for dinner at Brandon's house with his family. We had a lovely evening and Dawn invited Brandon and his wife to her wedding.

* * * * *

Randy called me after he read *Heal and Forgive.* My emotions ran very high, anticipating his comments. Although I no longer needed validation from my family, the confirmation Randy offered provided a new level of healing otherwise unavailable to me.

Randy told me that he *loved* the book, "I don't understand why you were afraid to have me read it?"

"What?" I questioned aloud as my uncontained shock and disbelief spilled over. "Are you kidding me? I thought that you would be angry at me for telling the family secret."

"Angry?" he inquired, "I don't understand why you held back. Why didn't you go into more detail about what really happened to us?"

At this point, I thought we were on some sort of alternate universe. Maybe I would wake up in the morning back in reality.

"Randy," I responded, "*Everyone* was angry any time I talked about the abuse."

Randy apologized. "The book opened my eyes about your relationship with Mom. I never understood your role as scapegoat. But," he continued, "the one thing that disturbed me the most and has stayed with me, was reading about the time of our separation."

We talked for hours. As our conversation wound down, I thanked Randy and told him that he had given me a wonderful gift. For days, the shock surrounding this unbelievable turn of events jumbled my thoughts—questioning which reality to believe. Randy offered comments that were in direct opposition to all my prior experiences.

A week or so later, Brandon gave me his feedback on the book. He reacted much the same as Randy—neither had understood my role as the scapegoat.

After standing alone in the truth about our family for over thirty-five years, it was difficult to fathom Randy and Brandon's positive reaction to my text or their willingness to understand my experiences. Although the book did precipitate discussions about painful past incidents and the consequences of those events, our conversations were also peppered with recollections of fun childhood antics and mischievous activities.

My brothers and I shared a history—some of it was good, some bad, but nonetheless it was a history that we alone had in common.

A business trip brought Randy back to Seattle in October. Tara and Dawn loved their Uncle Randy and excitedly anticipated our Thursday night gathering at a local restaurant for dinner. We filled the evening with laughter, old stories, and new accounts of our lives. Happy that Randy would once again be a part of our lives, Dawn extended him an invitation to her wedding. The evening ended too soon—leaving us longing for more.

I left for home with the realization that it was good to yearn for a greater connection. Better to long for more than to jeopardize the relationship by moving too fast.

CHAPTER SIXTEEN

"Hi, Honey. It's Mom."

We never know what the future holds.
Sometimes, the impossible happens.
—the author

From the moment my receptionist buzzed my office and I heard the words, "Hi, Honey, this is Mom," time held no meaning. It had been fourteen years since we had spoken. Randy telephoned me shortly after I talked to Mom. I barely remember my conversation with him. I don't remember much of what happened at work in the hours subsequent to Mom's call. I left work knowing that it was important to sort out my thoughts and to be present with my emotions. After returning to work the next morning, the day-to-day happenings in my life remained at an emotional distance for at least a few days.

From the quiet of my home, I reviewed my conversation with Mom—trying to make sense of her words.

For the first time in my life, Mom acknowledged my abuse, apologized, and expressed a desire to see me again. She also apologized for excluding me from the Lake. Hearing the words, "I'm sorry," provided a new level of healing and forgiveness previously unavailable without Mom's participation.

She offered a gift many estranged people will never receive. Although we all have the opportunity to reconcile the past for ourselves, we have no control over the willingness of our family members to reconcile our pasts together. Therefore, for many, no matter how much we heal ourselves, reconciliation is not possible. Mom told me that she had not read my entire book, but she had read excerpts and she was happy that I used my experiences to help others. Her words were shocking, to say the least, and left me with many questions.

Mom never told me what prompted her call, but she did say that she struggled through the recent family funeral, feeling the ramifications of our separation with deep despair. "I always figured that you and your brothers would get together after I died. They miss you and it's time for our family to come together," she uttered softly. "We all have a hole in our hearts."

I needed a period of transition to square years of abuse, mistreatment, and estrangement with the unsolicited apology Mom extended. My body and mind required a recovery phase and absorption time before I could have any more contact with my family or additional stimulation to my already overwhelmed psyche. After years of identifying myself as a motherless daughter, this new revelation was akin to the resurrection of a departed loved one.

Although I was at a moment of uncertainty in my life, of one fact, I was sure—it took a great deal of courage for Mom to call me.

* * * * *

Just as with premature forgiveness, there are certainly dangers associated with premature reconciliation. Healing first is the basis for successful resolution. Many people feel external or internal pressure to reconcile too soon—thereby sabotaging all chances for success.

I've heard from people who feel desperate to reunite when a family member becomes ill, their parents age, or out of guilt or pressure from others. We may be anxious for reconciliation out of a need to receive the nurturing we have always longed for, or to fill the void. No matter how much we desire reuniting with those from whom we are estranged, our family members may be unable or unwilling to have a relationship.

Unless we have healed enough to move past our anger, the time is not suitable for reconciliation. If we can't trust ourselves enough to provide our own safety, we are not safe enough to see a parent who has abused us. Reuniting is not possible if we haven't broken old patterns of behaving and responding. We need to be strong enough to maintain our own boundaries and separate identity, or we run the risk of causing further damage to our psyche.

Whereas love and hate share the same side of the emotional coin, indifference rests on the other side. This isn't to say that I didn't love my mother. If I hadn't loved her, she would not have been able to hurt me so deeply or angered me as much. However, it was the process of healing and separation that freed me from my emotional bondage and enabled healthy indifference. Healing, self-nurturing, and internalizing my worth and independence were required for me to feel indifferent to and unaffected by negative messages from my mother.

At first, I sat alone with my feelings—I didn't want additional input from other individuals added into my already over-stimulated mind. When I did begin to share my mother's phone call with supportive persons in my life, some people were simply thrilled to hear of my news; others were excited, but confused and wary; many were concerned for my well-being—they were afraid I'd be hurt again. Yet, I believed that I was strong enough to respond appropriately to any old patterns or issues that could crop up once I dealt with my confusion.

For my own protection, I needed the initial acknowledgment and apology Mom offered for my abuse or a relationship would not have been possible for me. Beyond that, I didn't need to rehash anything with her all over again. As long as we could have a relationship in the present, free from abuse, I was open to starting fresh and getting to know my mother again—slowly.

It was important to take "baby steps"—to proceed gradually as we rebuilt trust. Forgiveness was one thing; trust is another. Preparing for the possibility that old patterns would most likely present themselves shored me up. The challenge for me was to differentiate between primal "my survival is at stake" childhood triggers and the occasional present-day hurt feelings.

After Mom had apologized for my abuse during our phone conversation, she added, "But you are very stubborn and you handled the abuse differently from your brothers."

Reaping the rewards of hard work and healing, I felt strong and proud that her comments no longer injured me. Healing afforded me the ability to differentiate between re-living past hurts and my current experience. Was my mother's apology genuine? Yes, I believe it was. It *felt* genuine when she said it. True, she prematurely shared her experience after acknowledging mine—but I can live with that.

Prior to healing, Mom's comment would have left me devastated, desperately seeking her understanding and approval. In the past, the "child me" relived the times I pleaded with Mom to protect me from Ed, only to have her scream, "Why do I always have trouble with you—only you—never the boys?"

Contrary to my prior reactions, with a proud smile, I said to myself, "Damn straight, I'm stubborn. My stubbornness has served me well; it gave me the determination to heal and to break the cycle of abuse. I'm proud that I 'handled our abuse differently' and stood in the truth about our mistreatment." Hearing myself say those words infused me with courage. Mom's responses had nothing to do with me; they were all about her! Suddenly, my life changed forever. I didn't need my mother's approval. I *felt* it for myself—not just intellectually, but confidently from within.

"Yes," was my simple response to her comment about my stubbornness.

During our conversation, I expressed a different experience surrounding our final conversation fourteen years earlier. Although Mom quickly became defensive, I responded matter-of-factly, "I'm sure that was your experience."

We proceeded past the tension. My internal parent watched over me. I didn't know, until I spoke with Mom, that I had internalized a mother not just in theory but also in practice.

As painful as it was—estrangement afforded me the opportunity to heal from my abuse and find some peace in my life. In the beginning of our estrangement, I looked at our conflicts and only considered my experience. I needed to do this to build a foundation for healing.

Without discussing the past with my mother, I have a better understanding of both of our experiences. They are quite different; yet, to me, it doesn't matter, because today I am safe and I keep proper boundaries.

My childhood experience was one of abuse and longing for protection. It seems clear to me that everyone has the right to protect him or herself from severe abuse.

Whether I like it or not, Mom's experience was that I kept causing turmoil in her marriages by "complaining" about the abuse in the family. As skewed as this may seem to me, I do agree that this *was* her experience. My complaints *did* cause turmoil in her marriages.

My experience was that I needed to estrange from Mom for my very survival, but regardless of my reasons, her experience was that she was hurt and angry that I cut her out of my life for *any* reason. Not on this day, but later, it occurred to me—Mom had forgiven me too.

Understanding both these perspectives aids my ability to heal our relationship.

* * * * *

When other people worried that my mother would continue to blame and mistreat me, I assured them that although I didn't yet trust my mother, I had healed enough to trust myself to safeguard my own well-being. One confidant validated my stance with a wonderful analogy. He said, "Oh, it's kind of like a martial artist walking through a dangerous neighborhood. Even though danger is present, he knows he is safe because he can depend upon his own abilities."

"Yeah, it's like that," I said with a smile.

Weeks later, Brandon and Randy both relayed to me their astonishment that Mom had called me. Randy said, "I wanted to give you some time before I called again. I didn't want to overwhelm you. When I heard that Mom called you, I was in such a state of shock that I couldn't imagine how it affected you."

A few days after we spoke, I received an e-mail from Mom asking if Tara, Dawn, and I could meet her for dinner. We made plans to meet at a restaurant in a couple of weeks.

Although the girls welcomed the opportunity to become re-acquainted with their grandmother, they shared many of the conflicting emotions and caution that consumed my mind. Tara and Dawn both expressed their uneasiness that my mother had hurt them too. They tempered their optimism for reuniting with realistic concerns.

Tara had a personal emergency the day we were to meet with my mother. She asked me to tell her grandmother that she wanted to get together with her another time.

As Dawn and I readied ourselves for dinner with my mother, we spent a moment in prayer. We prayed for my mother, for ourselves and for guidance.

As we approached the restaurant, I saw Mom waiting alone in a chair. She looked sad. Her pain-filled expression deepened as she said to Dawn, "You're all grown up."

Mom's words set the tone for the evening. Without directly speaking of our loss, we mourned what should have been, what could have been, and the time that was lost.

With outstretched arms, I asked my mother for a hug and we embraced. I stood before her as a strong, confident, quietly powerful woman. For the first time in my life, in the presence of my mother, I was no longer a damaged child.

We had an enjoyable evening as we caught up on our lives as if we were old friends. Mom purposefully extended herself to us, offering copies of documents procured on her trip to Ellis Island, where she researched my paternal grandparents' entrance into the United States. I felt an ever-present sadness in my mother, and I hoped for further healing in our lives.

The evening went by quickly. As we walked to our cars, Mom said, "It was good to see you." She added with heartbreaking emotion, "Are you willing to see me again?"

Dawn and I responded in sympathetic unison, "Yes!"

I asked Mom for another hug and we watched as she slowly walked into the distance.

Each time I had contact with one of my family members, I needed recovery time to absorb a wide range of conflicting emotions: sadness, joy, uncertainty, hope, sorrow, and issues of trust. Contrary to the old ways, of "powering" through each event, I remained present with my feelings, staying true to myself and let my well-being guide me.

* * * * *

Within a few short months, I mourned the death of a family member and two old friends. At the same time, I experienced many conflicting emotions over the renewed relationships with two of my brothers, and my mother, and the excitement of Dawn's upcoming nuptials. Dawn's wedding would be on December 16, exactly one month after our dinner with my mother. To say I had a lot on my plate would be an understatement.

Although we were already at the brink of our emotional capabilities, a large part of me longed for my mother to be invited to the wedding. My daughters and I embraced the chance to become reacquainted with my mother. Nonetheless, we didn't believe we had the emotional reserves necessary to juggle all these new situations as quickly as required to invite Mom to the ceremony. Dawn's wedding was a once in a lifetime event and our emotional energy needed to remain focused on her joyous occasion. We knew our best opportunity for a successful reunion was to give ourselves enough time and energy to move forward with my mother in the healthiest manner possible.

Three days after we met for dinner, Mom called to wish me a happy birthday. Another unexpected surprise! We had a pleasurable conversation, and yet it was more than two months before we spoke again.

CHAPTER SEVENTEEN

Navigating Slippery Slopes

By early December, I had yet to have any contact with Rob. One evening, while rummaging through a room for a misplaced item, I came across a miniature version of the Hasbro toy, A Barrel of Monkeys, and I thought of Rob. As children, we had played our own creative version of A Barrel of Monkeys. With a chuckle, I mailed him this "symbol" of our inside joke in an effort to break the ice.

Randy, Brandon and I continued to enjoy frequent telephone conversations and visits. We amused ourselves with countless humorous memories, sharing a common history while bonding once again.

The beginning stages of rebuilding relationships with my brothers proved to be both fun and tense for me. Fear of the unknown left me worried about becoming rejected once more.

By the time Dawn walked down the aisle, I had begun to build some trust with Randy and Brandon. Reflecting back over the past three months, my emotional progress played like a movie on fast-forward. My original fears and confusion subsided. I found myself believing I might be able to return "home" again.

Brandon and Mares—along with Randy, Stacy, and their children—all attended Dawn's wedding. Just as when I met Brandon's children, it was both sad and sweet for me when I met Randy's children for the very first time.

Seeing Brandon and Randy again was like recapturing a lost part of my history and myself. Yet as would be expected, at times there were slippery slopes to navigate. While Randy was in Seattle for the wedding, he and his family had an early Christmas celebration with Brandon's family, Rob's daughter, and with Mom. Naturally, I had feelings of continued exclusion, just as Mom may have felt by not being at the wedding, and yet, I understood that it would take time for all of us to work through issues surrounding our estrangement and reconciliation.

The most difficult situation for me to journey through was the property at the lake. Randy and his family live in the family summer home for about six weeks each year and he stays at the Lake during his other visits from California. Because the Lake is central to their lives, they commented on events surrounding the summer home during most of our discussions.

Each time the Lake came up in conversation, it cut through me like a knife. The Lake was the "elephant" in the living room. Nobody spoke about the injustice surrounding my exclusion, and they acted as if nothing was out of the ordinary.

The first time Randy invited me to the Lake, I told him that I wasn't comfortable going there and we simply made alternate plans for our visit. The second time Randy suggested that we meet at the summer home, I repeated my feelings of discomfort.

Following a significant pause, I stated matter-of-factly, "I'm surprised that you don't get that. I'll never go to the Lake. After all the promises that were made to us since we were children, I think I was screwed when it comes to the Lake. I don't even like hearing about it. It's like rubbing salt in my wounds and it cuts me deep."

Randy responded with pain in his voice, "That's not my intention."

"I know," I replied.

"The reason Rob called you a few years ago was that it didn't seem right to us," he continued.

We both sat silently for a moment before Randy spoke again, "I don't know what to say. Am I wrong to hope that we can all enjoy the Lake together?"

After another uncomfortable silence I said, "Tell me, Randy, after what we were promised since we were kids, if you were excluded, would you go to the Lake?"

He paused for a moment before he replied, "I can get that."

When we hung up the phone, I sat with my hurt, sadness, and discomfort—remaining true to my feelings. My decisions were based on what was best for me and unlike before, I *knew* I had a right to my pain without permission from anyone. For the first time in my life, I felt like a grown-up even in the presence of my family. What a huge step.

As is common with adult children of abuse, I had ignored my feelings in the past and betrayed myself. I allowed re-injury in order to maintain or re-establish relationships. However, experience taught me that in order to continue to heal and forgive, I had to be free from the anxiety of re-injury and place my safety within myself.

Prior to our reconciliation, I dealt with my anger over my exclusion from the Lake. Other individuals acknowledged my injury—they helped me to discharge my anger and mourn my loss. My responsibility rested in not allowing re-injury and not partaking in this injustice, no matter the consequences.

Fortunately, my healing and emotional work afforded me a break from old patterns. Had I followed the old model and returned to the Lake as a "guest," I would have felt terribly injured and resentful, while the rest of my family plodded along merrily. Ignoring my feelings surrounding this major issue would have been addressing the Lake from a position of weakness and would have manifested itself in unhealthy ways. Resentment has a way of simmering until it boils over with hurt, angry words that long for understanding and recognition of the injustice.

My old ways of coping with wrongs would be to "hope" my brothers would "get it" and demonstrate concern for my feelings until it was too late. I'd feel re-victimized, while thinking to myself, see, they still don't care about me. Instead, I dealt from a position of strength and placed my well-being in my own hands. I allowed my brothers to share my discomfort without depending upon them to be considerate of my feelings. I honored my own feelings, protected myself, and did not go to the Lake. This isn't to say that I didn't mourn my exclusion from my father's estate all over again. I did. I mourned deeply.

CHAPTER EIGHTEEN

Preconceived Notions

Be open to learning new lessons
even if they contradict the lessons you learned yesterday.
—Ellen Degeneres in *Elle*

Randy and his family toured my business on their way to
the airport four days after Dawn's wedding, giving us one
last opportunity to say good-bye. That evening, just days
before Christmas, Brandon called to tell me that his wife
had just delivered their third child. The next day I went to
the hospital, thrilled to meet my beautiful new niece.

We experienced a bustling holiday season, filled with
new beginnings. As the road to reconciliation continued,
Rob sent me a thank you note for the "monkeys."

As we became more attached, I began to worry once
again that my renewed relationship with Randy wouldn't
last. During our final conversation fourteen years earlier, I
explained to Randy my decision to "divorce" myself from
Mom and my desire for a continued relationship with him.
Randy expressed his concerns, "I'm a little uncertain. I'm
afraid that you'll want me to divorce Mom too."

Picking up my end of the conversation, I assured him,
"I understand that Randy, and that's not what I want. I
want you to live your life the way that is comfortable for

you and for you to have the relationships you want with anyone. I'll support whatever you choose. I'm asking the same. I'm asking you to support my decision to divorce Mom. I just want to have a relationship with you without becoming dragged back into the family dysfunction."

By the time we finished our conversation, I thought we had successfully negotiated a new relationship. I was both stunned and saddened when we didn't speak for fourteen years.

In early January 2007, after an enjoyable telephone conversation with Randy, I called him back and told him I was worried he would stop seeing me again. "Nahhh," was his reply. "We had a misunderstanding before and it won't happen again."

To his credit, Randy e-mailed me later explaining what he meant by misunderstanding. His recollection of our final conversation was he believed that if he continued to see Mom, I wouldn't see him. I was stunned. It took a while for this information to sink into my mind. Randy really thought he had to choose. I was so saddened. I couldn't believe we lost fourteen years over a simple misunderstanding.

I am very grateful Randy had the courage to tell me his experience. As I churned over this new information all night, unanswered questions began to make sense to me. Then I realized that healthy families don't lose fourteen years over a simple misunderstanding. Our "simple misunderstanding" was the result of decades of embedded family patterns that colored all of our perceptions. All those years ago, despite my reassurances, Randy was certain I asked him to choose between Mom and me. Today, that makes sense. Randy viewed me from my assigned role as the family scapegoat/troublemaker, making it unable for him to hear my words. Family perceptions dictated that Nancy "divided" the family.

After Randy stopped talking to me, my history of rejection prevented me from calling Randy and asking him why he wasn't talking to me anymore. The rejection had knocked the wind out of me and I was too "broken" to pursue him further. Because our perceptions were so well rooted, we simply let our preconceived notions stand rather than questioning one another's true intent. He thought I offered him an ultimatum. I thought we negotiated a new relationship—one in which Mom was a part of Randy's life, but not a part of my life. We unknowingly had completely different experiences.

Randy and I each endeavored to recover from our abuse and family history the best way we knew how. Given where each one of us was on our healing journey, I don't believe we could have responded any other way. It's important for me to understand our family history so history doesn't repeat itself, but rather offers me the ability to feel and live in the present.

I appreciated Randy's wisdom and foresight when he told me, "I am pursuing our relationship with my eyes wide open, knowing that there will be some difficult times that are well worth the rewards." As he said, "We can't change the past; however, we are in complete control of our futures."

It is important for me to find a balance. Every time Randy and I share difficult emotional work, I need some fun time with him. After we worked through this issue, I called him back and said, "Can Randy come out and play?"

* * * * *

Time passed, allowing me the opportunity to adjust to my new feelings and to settle back into a normal routine. Mom is again in a long-term relationship, but this time with a very nice family-oriented man. Two months after we last spoke, I sent Mom and her gentleman friend an invitation to dinner, along with directions to my house.

Had I not healed the child within, the intervening time since our last conversation would have left me needy and insecure, desperate for reassurance that Mom wanted me in her life, and it would have damaged our possibility for success. However, I was comfortable with our pace and aware that Mom must have been struggling with her own issues surrounding reconciliation as well.

Mom is very intelligent. She is knowledgeable in many areas, especially in matters concerning history, business, literature, and current events. Yet she isn't one to share her feelings. I don't believe my mother is comfortable with the intimate language of emotion that often binds women in their relationships. Nonetheless, she enjoys the sharing of events, typically found in the company of men. In a mother-daughter relationship, this can leave the daughter feeling alone and distanced from the mother.

However, I no longer anticipated the stereotypical mother-daughter relationship. As we began to spend time together, I realized that, although my mother was still emotionally unavailable, we could enjoy occasional get-togethers based on a historical bond and respect for one another's differences.

I needed time apart from my mother to heal my own life before I could see her through new eyes. I view her not as just the woman who gave me life, but as a separate individual with her own wounded places and her own style of loving. She may not have loved me the way I needed her to as a child, yet I do believe that she loves me.

I saw my mother recently at my nephew's birthday party. Mom stood on the sidelines and took hundreds of digital snapshots as the rest of us laughed and played. I'm grateful I had healed enough to recognize the loving connection she made through her pictures. As we sat together at the end of the party and viewed all the images, I realized that Mom shared her love not through words and interaction, but it shined through to me nonetheless.

CHAPTER NINETEEN

As Time Marches On

Growth is the only evidence of life.
—John Henry Newman

By February 2007, the reconciliation with my family felt rather anti-climactic. The lack of emotional euphoria was, to coin a Martha Stewart phrase, "A Good Thing."

I recognize that this may sound odd to you. Indeed, to the less-healed me who cried out for a mommy fourteen years earlier, an anti-climactic reunion would have sounded "cold." The less-healed me needed emotional connection *with* my mother and safety *from* my mother. Yet, the healed me found "anti-climactic" wonderful. Anti-climactic meant that I was no longer enmeshed with my family. During our necessary separation, I went to work on the job my mother started. I mothered myself.

I enjoy my visits with my family; yet, I have my own life and my own sense of self, separate from everyone else.

When I truly honored my feelings through each stage of my recovery, my outlook ended up changing dramatically and my emotional-self moved forward in ways that I would have never believed.

There was a time in my life when forgiveness was premature. I didn't think I would ever forgive. Therefore, I understand those who have not healed adequately to forgive, and those who have. Both places in my life were equally important steps in my journey towards healing.

In much the same way, up until my mother called me and apologized, I didn't think *anything* could or would ever happen that would precipitate feeling safe enough to be willing to explore a relationship with her again. The thought of reconciliation seemed too unsafe and frightening to attempt. I also resented the thought of risking my safety for the sake of an artificial relationship.

When I was a young woman, it was difficult to live with the desire to have a relationship with my mother, when she was unable to meet my needs. Amidst a life wrought with abuse, Mom and I did not share an emotional connection. Throughout my relationship with my mother, she stated, "The sharing of feelings has no place in relationships—they only 'mess things up.'"

As long as I had expectations of emotional connectedness, I set myself up for disappointment. During a lifetime of emotional estrangement and our fourteen-year physical estrangement, I experienced a great deal of grief associated with accepting that whether we had a relationship or not, Mom and I would never share an emotional connection.

Fourteen years earlier, I hadn't understood that our lack of connection couldn't be "fixed." If Mom had extended herself in an attempted reconciliation back then, anti-climatic is not what I would have imagined or needed. I would have jumped right back into enmeshment with the hopeful excitement that Mom would finally give me what I needed. Isn't that what moms are supposed to do?

During our early separation, I desired a return to my enmeshed family system, but one "tweaked" to be supportive and understanding. I believed that in order to reconcile with Mom, we needed to "rehash" the past. I wanted her to listen with an eagerness to understand my experience and to ease my pain, to apologize, to replace the bad with the good, and to provide *for* me a safe relationship with her. As the estrangement from my mother progressed, I didn't want a relationship if I had to "settle" for anything less. I didn't take into account all of the emotional growth I had accomplished in the intervening years.

Today, my internal parent provides much of the nurturing the less-healed me desired from my mother and the rest of my family. I no longer need help from my family with healing, validation, forgiveness, understanding, nurturing, or safety, because I receive this help from other individuals in my life. My internal parent is strong enough to stop seeking help where it is unavailable. If I still felt compelled to seek understanding where it doesn't exist, I wouldn't be ready to reconcile. In this regard, individuating from my mother enabled my reconciliation.

Reconciliation is not possible for everyone. I know some people who experience continued physical, sexual, and emotional violence in their families to a degree that prohibits any safe contact. For these adult children, their internal parent protects them from further harm by maintaining their separation. Other estranged individuals may have healed adequately to desire reconciliation, only to find family members unwilling to see them.

Whether we forgive or don't forgive, whether we reconcile or remain apart from our families, healing is vital for our own happiness and well-being.

My life is much the same as it was during the estrangement, but it feels better.

In many small but meaningful ways, Mom has shown her affection for me, such as taking a seat next to mine at a gathering, or calling just to say, "Hi." These simple gestures have not gone unnoticed. Mom's subtle efforts to make peace with the past help to put old wounds to rest.

I have enjoyed occasional get-togethers and contact that augments my life positively. Not only have I enjoyed interactions with my family of origin, but I also relish time with my nieces and nephews.

My brother's children are bundles of energy—full of rambunctious excitement and laughter. With my own children grown, I delight in sharing occasional childhood events—visiting the zoo through a child's eyes, full of innocence and wonder, for instance. The energy and enthusiasm they exude retelling childhood experiences at school, with friends or at dance class amuses me.

The process of reconciliation has been healing for me. I have experienced emotional growth that would not have been possible without the opportunity to revisit my family dynamics from a more healed perspective.

Randy and I shared numerous conversations about our lives, our family and our experiences. By May 2007, thirteen months after his initial e-mail, Randy said, "Although the rest of the family says that they still don't trust you, I'm jumping into our relationship with both feet."

I anticipated continuing to build on our new foundation when Randy and his family would come to Washington for their annual summer stay. I didn't foresee that our nearly weekly conversations would come to a halt or that we would spend only a few hours together during the summer.

Again, because the family summer home is central to their lives, the family spent their time focused on activities surrounding the Lake, which left little room for activities and people such as me, away from the Lake.

Through my conversations with Randy and Brandon, I learned that although the rest of the family was never physically estranged—they were not particularly close. They spent little time together outside of summertime and were not one another's "safe place to fall." The Lake is their common bond and I am not included in that bond.

At first, I revisited my feelings of hurt and injustice, and my sense of rejection and exclusion. Mostly, I was just sad—sad because whether they were in my life or not—we would remain at an emotional distance.

I had to remind myself not to seek support "where it wasn't" and to seek support from where it was. I knew my family didn't understand my experience. I'd already had a conversation about the Lake with Randy months earlier and more recently with Brandon.

During a telephone conversation, I told Brandon I had just cut down some trees on my property at home. "If you have some extra wood you'd like taken off of your hands, could I have some?" he inquired.

"If you'd like," I began. "Do you burn wood at home?"

"No, it's for the Lake. We have a little wood there, but not very much. So if you have some to spare that would be great!"

Ouch! A shot through the heart.

As Brandon continued to talk about the goings on at the Lake, I listened quietly while formulating in my mind just how to respond. Finally, he said, "Hello! Are you there?"

"I'm here. I'm just not comfortable giving you wood for the Lake," I responded. "I'm not a part of that so it isn't comfortable for me."

"I can understand that," was Brandon's reply.

It seemed odd to me that my family simultaneously "understood" and didn't understand. Reconciliation doesn't necessarily mean that all family dynamics have changed, but I have.

"Happily ever after" does not necessarily mean a storybook ending. "Happily ever after" can mean accepting what is—as what is. I love my family members and I believe they love me too. I take the good they have to offer and reject the bad, while I remind myself of all I have to be grateful for: my partner, my friends, my kids, my aunt—all the people who provide joy in my life and a "safe place to fall."

I'm sure there will always be trials to navigate; yet, I accept my family members for who they are—understanding that we all are doing the best we know how. Thus far, mine has been a long road to travel. Yet, I look forward in time with realistic optimism. Who knows what the future holds? What I do know is this: today I continue to live an abuse-free life, and my well-being is firmly in my own hands.

CHAPTER TWENTY

Is the Time Right for Reconciliation?

Reconciliation is everyone recognizing and treating each other as equals, and everyone must be responsible for their own actions.
—Pauline Hanson

Some individuals may never be ready to reconcile with estranged family members. I know a woman who moved across the country, unlisted her phone number and started life anew only to have her violent family members track her down, stalk her, and interfere with her new job, friends and neighbors.

I have heard from other people who deeply desire reconciliation with a parent or sibling, but they simply cannot put themselves in harm's way for the sake of a relationship. As painful as estrangement is, these individuals must somehow learn to live with a separation that feels like the "lesser of two evils."

Many people do wish to reconcile with family members only to face repeated rejection. A number of individuals have asked me, "What can I do to reconcile with my family?"

Healing first is the basis for successful resolution. Once you have healed adequately—you are free to explore the present. Most people I'm acquainted with, who have successfully mended an estrangement, didn't go back and re-hash specific events from the past. This is why healing on your own is so important. With my own mother for instance, she acknowledged my "abuse," in general. She did this on her own initiative and that was the last we spoke of it. We placed our desire on a new kind of relationship. This opened the door for me to explore if the abuse had become a thing of the past.

But what if you reach out and the other person still wants to avoid you?

Give the message that you are accessible. You could send an occasional note, birthday card, or e-mail expressing your openness to a relationship if and when he or she is ready to reconnect.

Often, no matter how much we desire reuniting with those from who we are estranged, our family members may be unable or unwilling to have a relationship. As difficult as this may seem, there is nothing you can do to convince him or her to see you. Beyond keeping the door open, find support to help you accept estrangement and move on to live the best life possible.

As painful as estrangement is, you can use the time to grow in ways that may not be possible while having a relationship with your family members. My greatest emotional growth occurred as a result of my separation from my mother. Estrangement forced me to develop my own sense of self, separate from my family.

If one attempts reconciliation too soon—while still angry, for instance—failure could further cement bad feelings and complicate the process when conditions are more favorable.

Anger often bleeds through into a relationship, which makes success difficult at best. Unresolved anger—on either side—could erupt without warning or sabotage your progress with passive aggressive behaviors.

When I was still angry with my mother, I thought I needed her to help me move past my anger. Nonetheless, I knew I couldn't count on her to help me heal. It is human nature to focus on the behavior of the other individual—hoping they will change—especially in cases of abuse. I knew I had to focus on my own healing journey separate from my mother. This required time apart from her, in the company of supportive friends, in therapy and on my own to find constructive ways to deal with and move past my anger.

Sometimes, we are so desperate to have a relationship that we try to do *their* emotional work for them. We think to ourselves, if I could only get them to see "this" or "that" we will get along.

Other times, we think that if we "jump through hoops" to please them, they will love us.

I know a man who reached out to care for his dying father. Although he felt internal pressure to resolve the relationship before his dad died, their eleventh-hour reconciliation didn't work. This left my friend angry and bitter—cementing his hurt feelings even twenty years later.

Before considering reconciliation with a family member, ask yourself if conditions are favorable:

- Am I still angry with him or her?
- Is my family member still angry with me?

- Am I the same as I was at the time of the estrangement?

- Is my family member the same as they were at the time of the estrangement?

- Is continued physical, sexual, or emotional violence present in my family?

- Will I have to sacrifice my well-being for the sake of this relationship?

- Am I emotionally enmeshed with my family?

- Do I feel the need to engage and "change" his or her perceptions?

- Do I feel pressured in any way, either internally or externally to reconcile? This could be out of guilt, cultural or religious pressure, family illness, aging parents or enmeshment.

If the answer to any one of these questions is "Yes," it's probably not a good time to reconcile.

My answers to these questions changed over the period of time I was cut off from my family.

	Beginning stages of estrangement	Later stages of estrangement	At time of reconciliation
1. Am I still angry?	Yes	No	No
2. Are they still angry?	Yes	Yes	Don't know
3. Am I the same?	Yes	No	No
4. Are they the same?	Yes	Yes	Don't know
5. Is continued abuse present?	Yes	Don't know	No
6. Will I have to sacrifice myself?	Yes	Yes	No

7. Am I enmeshed with my family?	Yes	Partially	No
8. Do I need to "engage" in old arguments?	Yes	Yes	No
9. Do I feel pressured to reconcile?	Yes	No	No

If the answers to the above questions are "No," you may still want to consider the following questions. There are no "right" or "wrong" answers, only points to consider that may aid in your individual family circumstances and journey. Some of these questions are difficult and run deep. The answers are only between you and yourself:

- Do I really want to reconcile?
- Does he or she want to reconcile?
- Am I strong enough to handle the possibility of rejection?
- Have I grown emotionally and changed since we last spoke?
- Has he or she grown and changed?
- Do I need an apology?
- Can I accept an apology?
- Do they need an apology?
- Can I extend an apology?
- Do I forgive him or her?
- Does he or she forgive me?
- Am I ready to move forward?
- Is he or she ready to move forward?
- Can I take full responsibility for my own safety and well-being?

- Am I able to set and maintain appropriate boundaries?

- Do I know how to respond differently to old, unhealthy family patterns?

- Am I able to maintain my own separate identity independent from my family such as: choice of mate, religious beliefs, sexuality, political beliefs, education, career, relationships, activities and parenting style?

- Has there been a "power shift"—equalizing the relationship?

- Have I healed sufficiently to differentiate between old painful experiences and the occasional present hurt feelings?

- Have I healed enough to know that his or her responses to me are about him or her and not about me?

- Am I indifferent to negative comments?

- Have I already built a good life separate from my family of origin?

- Have I developed my own family traditions?

- Do I have a supportive "family of choice?"

- Do I have an attitude of gratitude for the good already in my life?

- Am I open to therapy with my family?

- Is my family open to therapy with me?

You may also wish to consider what sort of new relationship you desire with your family member(s).

Do I merely want a truce and a cordial relationship? A friendship? Or something deeper?

If you believe the time may be right to reconcile—move slowly. Take baby steps while you begin to build trust—both in yourself and with your relatives.

Start out accentuating the positive. Find common ground. Reminisce about good memories, share mutual interests, and express positive feelings.

I developed a different relationship with each family member, including varying degrees of closeness. Independently, we each defined fresh connections and new communication styles.

My brother Randy and I started out with a few short e-mails, and then talked on the telephone before we saw each other in person. Our first visit was five months after Randy's initial e-mail and was very brief. It is much easier to move forward slowly than it is to try to pull back if we have moved too fast.

If you have been estranged from your entire family, rather than "jumping" right back in and seeing all of them at once, you may want to consider staggering separate visits.

During the first thirteen months since Randy's initial e-mail to me, we enjoyed frequent telephone conversations and saw each other a few times. Brandon and I also talked on the phone and took pleasure in occasional get-togethers. My mother and I communicated periodically via phone, e-mail, and saw each other in person on only four different occasions. Rob and I e-mailed one another a couple of times, spoke on the phone once (April 30), yet had not seen one another in person. We each began developing separate relationships in our own time and in our own way, without getting together all at once.

This pace may seem slow to you; yet, it feels healthy.

At first, keep your time short and don't discuss difficult issues that come up with your family until you have had time to work through intense emotions alone or with supportive friends. In the beginning, when negative feelings came up for me, I said, "Ouch!" to myself and waited until I had enough time to work through the issue before I talked to my family members again. Spend time in between visits adjusting to and absorbing the many positive and negative conflicting emotions you will experience by sharing with trusted confidants: a therapist, a minister, friends, and/or support groups.

Expect to navigate some slippery slopes and develop ways to help you cope with new situations. You may want to limit the length of your visits at first and insulate yourself by not spending one-on-one time with a family member if you don't feel safe.

After attempting reconciliation, you may be satisfied with the results and you may not. You can only control your half of the relationship.

My brother Randy was the catalyst behind our family reconciliation. Without Randy's initiative and Mom's courage to call me—reconciliation would not have transpired no matter how much I healed.

I know people who have tried to reconcile only to find themselves on the receiving end of continued abuse, which served to quiet any doubts that they may have had about their initial estrangement. In other words, they may have changed but their family member had not.

Others haven't undergone a substantial change and the reunion didn't succeed because they still need the type of relationship that their family member can't provide.

Even with willingness on both sides, communication can be fragile and undermine the best of intentions.

Having said all of that—many reconciliations do succeed. Some people are overjoyed with their renewed relationships, while others have "anti-climactic" reunions. Many individuals are simply happier and more content than they were before. Others may experience a cycle of emotions including all of the above.

Whether reconciliation succeeds or not, you will undoubtedly learn from the experience. Take heart in the unmistakable growth that occurs from all your emotional hard work.

Notes

PREFACE

Howard, Jane. *Families*. (Simon & Schuster, 1978).

CHAPTER ONE

Richards, Nancy. *Heal and Forgive: Forgiveness in the Face of Abuse*. (Nevada City: Blue Dolphin Publishing, Inc., 2005) pp. 3-12, 14-17, 25-29.

Vachss, Andrew. "You Carry the Cure in Your Own Heart." (New York: *Parade Magazine*, August 28, 1994) p. 4. On-line at www.vachss.com.

Lerner, Harriet Godhor, Ph.D. *The Dance of Anger: A Woman's Guide to Changing the Patterns of Intimate Relationships*. (New York: Harper & Row/Perennial Library, 1985) p. 188.

CHAPTER TWO

Richards, Nancy. pp. 21-22, 39-42, 45, 48, 102.

Fischer, Lucy Rose, Ph.D. *Linked Lives: Adult Daughters and Their Mothers*. (New York: Harper &Row, 1986) p.24.

CHAPTER THREE

Richards, Nancy. p. 56.

Marilyn Ferguson. http://thinkexist.com/quotation/ultimately_ we_know_deeply_that_the_other_side_of/216384.html

CHAPTER FOUR

Richards, Nancy. p. 57, 61-62, 89.

CHAPTER FIVE

Richards, Nancy. p. 27.

Herman, Judith Lewis. *Trauma and Recovery.* (New York: Basic Books, 1997) p.7.

CHAPTER SIX

Engels, Beverly. *Divorcing a Parent: Free Yourself from the Past and Live the Life You've Always Wanted.* (Ballantine, 1991) p. 103.

Secunda, Victoria. *When You and Your Mother Can't be Friends: Resolving the Most Complicated Relationship of Your Life.* (New York: Delta, 1990) pp. 358-359.

Sichel, Mark. *Healing from Family Rifts: Ten Steps to Finding Peace After Being Cut off from a Family Member.* (McGraw-Hill, 2004) p. xi.

Deepak Chopra. http://quotations.about.com/od/stillmorefamouspeople/a/DeepakChopra1.htm

CHAPTER SEVEN

Helen Keller. http://www.quotationspage.com/quote/1632.html

CHAPTER EIGHT

Sichel, Mark. p. 148

Engels, Beverly. p. 140.

Richards, Nancy. p. 101.

CHAPTER NINE

Pamela Glenconner. http://www.wisdomquotes.com/000708.html

Richards, Nancy. p. 43, 54.

William Arthur Ward. http://thinkexist.com/quotes/william_arthur_ward/2.html

Kolb, Janice Gray. *Cherishing.* (Nevada City: Blue Dolphin Publishing, Inc., 2007) p. 4. Reprinted with permission from Blue Dolphin Publishing. Copyright 2007. All rights reserved.

CHAPTER TEN

Riklan, David & contributing author, Richards, Nancy. *101 Great Ways to Improve Your Life, Volume 2.* (Marlboro, NJ: Self Improvement Online, Inc., 2006) pp. 5-7. On-line at: http://www.selfgrowth.com/articles/Healing_Forgiving_and_Overcoming_Abuse.html

Horton, Anne L. & Williamson, Judith A., editors. *Abuse and Religion: When Praying Isn't Enough.* (Lexington, MA: Lexington Books, D.C. Heath and Company, 1988) as it appears in: Fortune, Marie M. *Violence in the Family—A Workshop Curriculum for Clergy and Other Helpers.* (Cleveland: Pilgrim Press, 1991) p. 174.

Lewis Smedes. http://www.brainyquote.com/quotes/quotes/l/lewisbsme132886.html

Richards, Nancy. pp. xxi, 115, 121.

Bishop Desmond Tutu. http://www.texansforpeace.org/Resources PeaceQuotations1.htm

CHAPTER ELEVEN

Nathaniel Branden. http://www.achieving-life-abundance.com/acceptance-quotes.html

Sichel, Mark. p.42.

CHAPTER TWELVE

Richards, Nancy. p. 120

CHAPTER FIFTEEN

Clara Ortega. http://www.quoteland.com/author.asp?AUTHOR_ID=1726

Mandela, Nelson. *The Long Walk to Freedom: The Autobiography of Nelson Mandela* (Little Brown Company; 1st edition, November 1994).

Chapter Nineteen

John Henry Newman. http://www.brainyquote.com/quotes/quotes/j/johnhenryn159080.html

CHAPTER TWENTY

Hanson, Pauline. http://www.brainyquote.com/quotes/quotes/p/paulinehan214702.html

About
Nancy Richards

Nancy Richards is the author of *Heal and Forgive: Forgiveness in the Face of Abuse* (Nevada City: Blue Dolphin Publishing, Inc., 2005) and co-author of *101 Great Ways to Improve Your Life, Volume 2* (Marlboro: Self Improvement Online, Inc., 2006).

Richards is an adult survivor of childhood abuse. She is the single parent of two adult daughters. Richards is a successful business woman, as vice president and general manager of a wholesale food processing company in Seattle. She makes her home in the greater Seattle area.

CPSIA information can be obtained at www.ICGtesting.com
Printed in the USA
LVOW121910130912

298705LV00001B/34/P